Audrey,

Thanks

friendship. +

From you and all that

you do.

Sharecropping

to Non-Stopping

This is my

story. Enjoy!

Margaret Hill

6 - 7 - 16

Blessings!

From Sharecropping *to* Non-Stopping

Reflections on Life from a Veteran Educator

Dr. Margaret Bynum Hill

FROM SHARECROPPING TO NON-STOPPING
REFLECTIONS ON LIFE FROM A VETERAN EDUCATOR

iUniverse books may be ordered through booksellers or by contacting:

iUniverse
1663 Liberty Drive
Bloomington, IN 47403
www.iuniverse.com
1-800-Authors (1-800-288-4677)

ISBN: 978-1-4917-6879-2 (sc)
ISBN: 978-1-4917-6880-8 (e)

Library of Congress Control Number: 2015909868

Print information available on the last page.

iUniverse rev. date: 8/31/2015

Contents

DEDICATION

This book is dedicated to all members of the Bynum/Willis family, especially my mother and father, Roosevelt and Sophia Willis Bynum.

Our world is so complex that it is difficult from time to time to determine what is best and how to move forward in life. I appreciate my siblings playing games with me after church on Sunday, after working in the fields during summer and after we completed our chores on Saturday. I appreciate getting to know many of my cousins, uncles and aunts, seeing them mostly at church as many of us did not attend the same schools. I'm thankful for my grandparents who allowed us to stay with them, including my mom and dad, when we were young. I'm thankful to my cousin, Randolph Peete, who gave me a lot of information about the family, information that I had

My father, Roosevelt Bynum and my mother, Sophia Willis Bynum.

never known even though I was an adult at the time. I'm thankful to Uncle Randall and Aunt Birdie Mae who took my sister and me into their home after our house burned to the ground. I'm thankful to Uncle Ryland and his son Kenneth who let us know that everybody in the family was not dark skinned and had kinky hair. I'm thankful to my cousin Hattie who kicked me out of her house and gave me a reality check at a young age. I'm thankful to my sister, Viola, who made my wedding dress for my first marriage. I appreciate all of my Bynum cousins because our distinct noses let everybody know we were related. I'm thankful for my brother Raymond who continues to make sure that my tenant pays on time and my house stays in good shape. I'm thankful to my brother Kenneth (Buddy) who made sure my car was always running since I couldn't afford a mechanic. I appreciate Linwood for naming me Babysis, a name that embarrassed me as a child but I learned how dear and precious it was as an adult. I'm thankful to Clasteen for... well, I'll think of something later. Finally, thanks to Robert Hill, my spouse, for his encouragement and support as I continue to support the community and youth.

To My Family

Friends are selected, family members are not
In spite of how we feel about each other,
Even though the decision was made without our input
It's a blessing to have every sister and brother.

I know God wants us to be good, if not great citizens
And has given us great opportunities in every way,
It is up to us to make the most of our lives
As we model good ethics, morals and values from day to day.

As I acknowledge the family names
Whether it's Bynum, Willis or another,
I thank you for being an intricate part of my life
But special thanks to Roosevelt, my father, and Sophia, my mother.

All six of us children worked, cried and played as a family
And enjoyed the farm as much as we could,
Many of our farm chores were left undone
But as sharecroppers, we felt we had done more than we should.

I made it off the farm, and had a pretty good life
Which will be shared in this book,
I've done my best to support any community that I lived in
A career in education and volunteerism was all it took.

My regrets are that my parents did not see my accomplishments
God called them to heaven to be by his side,
My mother passed at age fifty-four, and
my dad at age seventy-nine
My mind is still clear of the days they both died.

To my oldest sister, Viola and my middle brother, Kenneth
You also left us too early for the heaven above,
But don't think a day will ever go by
Where I will not forget your graceful love.

To the rest of the family, and you know who you are
We must be thankful for how well we look,
Now get your mind in shape and your credit card out
Then get to a store or online and order my book.

Left to right: Linwood, Clasteen, Margaret, and Raymond.

Foreword

By Anne Viricel

Like many in our region, I have been a longtime fan of Dr. Margaret Bynum Hill. She is a generous and thoughtful person with a no-nonsense approach to life daily delivered with kindness, tact, and respect even when she is facing a challenging individual or situation.

You can speak with Dr. Hill for just a short while and realize she is not only listening to you, she truly cares about what you have to say. And this unusual level of caring – a bit old fashioned in today's "Me-First" society – may well be what most draws such a wide variety of people to her. She is ever ready to give of herself (as her full-to-the-brim smartphone calendar demonstrates), and although she probably receives at least one well-deserved humanitarian award each month, I don't believe I've ever heard her boast about a single one. As a matter of fact, she was reticent to include photos of herself receiving awards unless they were particularly relevant to the storyline.

Dr. Hill clearly exemplifies what, I believe, Robert K. Greenleaf meant in his now-famous 1970 essay, *The Servant as Leader*.

"The servant-leader *is* servant first… It begins with the natural feeling that one wants to serve, to serve *first*. Then conscious choice brings one to aspire to lead. That person is sharply different from one who is *leader* first… The difference manifests itself in the care taken by the servant-first to make sure that other people's highest priority needs are being served. The best test, and difficult to administer, is: Do those served grow as persons? Do they, *while being served*, become healthier, wiser, freer, more autonomous, more likely themselves to become servants? *And*, what is the effect on the least privileged in society? Will they benefit or at least not be further deprived? A servant-leader focuses primarily on the growth and well-being of people and the communities to which they belong… The servant-leader shares power, puts the needs of others first and helps people develop and perform as highly as possible."

I've checked, and they were not acquainted, but should you complete this book and not think this is a case study in applied servant-leadership, I'd be surprised.

Simply stated, for Dr. Hill, it's not about improving her own position, it's about making life better for others. And although her singular focus has, on occasion, ruffled a feather or two, Dr. Hill knows that at the end of the day, it's the good we leave behind us that most genuinely defines the value of our lives.

It has been an honor and a privilege to get to know Dr. Hill through the preparation of her book. We spent many Friday afternoons deliberating how to cobble together hundreds of moments into a cohesive life story. Once we felt we had enough material and it was time to begin the serious process of writing, I admit to grieving the loss of those laughter-filled meetings. It is not often you get to spend time with an angel, but I did. And now you get to spend a little time with her, too. Enjoy.

ACKNOWLEDGMENTS

It was in 2002, I believe, when one of my teachers retired and suggested that I attend a writing class with her. I had not retired and had to remind her of that but did agree to attend the class once I was in retirement. Well there was no rest because Doris Anderson, retired English teacher with great writing skills, approached me again. I agreed since I knew she was not going to leave me alone.

When I started the class, the professor asked that we always bring a writing assignment to each meeting. I did not have any specific topic that I was interested in, but I always said to students that one day I should write a book about all of their excuses and school challenges. I decided to write about the students at San Andreas High School but thought, 'Uhmmmmmm, perhaps I should say something about my background.'

So, I started talking about being the daughter of sharecroppers and my early educational experiences. After reading my first assignment, the professor, Dr. Bruce McAllister, stopped me and said I need to write about me, not the students. We compromised and the rest is history.

In May, 2011, while attending a Gala, I heard Les Brown, motivational speaker, talk about how many of us go to our graves without telling our story and suggested that we all should write

...because we never know what affect it would have on someone else. I knew when I left that event, I would work on getting my writing published in a book called, "It's All About The Children." It was published in June 2011 and while many copies have been sold, more have been given away because I knew this was a story people should read.

One of my books was purchased by Dr. Anne Viricel who, for some reason, was fascinated about my life and wanted to know more. It was unbelievable when she asked if I would allow her to write a book about me, and for those who know Anne, know you always say yes. For more than eight months, we meet on Fridays – I clarified and answered questions and proudly gave additional information to Anne since my first book was just a synopsis of my life. I spoke – Anne wrote.

So, in summary, my acknowledgements go to the following people:

- Doris Anderson who insisted that I write whether I wanted to or not
- Dr. Bruce McAllister who thought my early childhood life was exciting while I thought it was boring
- Dr. Anne Viricel who visualized a movie, tv show, and/or an exciting bestseller in the making which is where we are starting with this project
- Everyone who read my first book and wanted to know when the next one would be published

We hope you enjoy reading my story as much as we enjoyed writing it.

CHAPTER ONE

Growing Up Bynum

Apples don't fall far from the tree, but neither do nuts.
~Margaret Hill

This is a story about my life.

It's quite a long story, but it's been quite a long life.

And I have no intention of having it end any time soon, although there have been some trials that I wonder if God put there just to test how serious I was about that.

Poet Ivy Baker Priest once wrote, "The world is round and the place which may seem like the end may also be only the beginning." So even though I have seen many years, I have yet to circumnavigate the world that will define my contribution to this life. And that thought brings me a special kind of joy.

It started quite some time ago a ways outside the town of Newsome in the State of Virginia. I was the fifth Bynum child born, and based on history of the family, I should've been the last. Linwood was the first born; Viola came two years and three months later. Then Kenneth Edward, who we called Buddy, was born 15 months after that. Clasteen, my closest sister, was born 19 months after Buddy. And 15 months later, I arrived.

It was a cold December day and Momma, who by that time was no stranger to childbirth, was getting horribly tired trying to bring me into the world.

Linwood, who was the one who told me the story of this auspicious day, said someone must have alerted Uncle Randall because he drove his mule and cart to Newsome, to get the doctor to assist the midwife with my delivery. He said Uncle Randall beat the mule to make it run as fast as possible to get the doctor back to the house.

He wasn't fast enough, though, as when he arrived, I had already joined my family and was wrapped in a blanket in my mother's arms. She told me later she'd stared at this new little bundle just wondering where in the world I'd gotten the reddish brown hair that would distinguish me from my brothers and sisters throughout my childhood.

After nearly two years with no other children born in the Bynum home, it was felt I would also be the last. Hence, I was tagged with the nickname "Babysis" although some say my oldest brother gave me that name because he couldn't say "Margaret."

Regardless, I was the cherished youngest child for six years, and although it was sometimes lonely when I could not join my siblings when they went to school, it was also an opportunity to spend time with my mother and father and to explore my world without the assistance of others.

But much to my surprise, one day this chubby little person, who did not look like Clasteen and my baby dolls, was suddenly in the house. It was my new brother, Raymond Clayton Bynum and he truly was the last child born into my immediate family.

I still vividly remember crying, and saying, "He cheated me out of being Babysis", the name that I'd grown to love. Years later,

Raymond Bynum, baby brother – today.

I would come to realize how my place in the family and the addition of this infant usurper would affect how I looked at the world.

Although I was not aware at the time, we were dirt poor, living in a wooden little house at the edge of the farm where my father was a sharecropper. I had a small child's simple chores, but until we were old enough to work on the farm, there wasn't a lot for me to do and there were no families with children my age nearby, so I spent considerable time playing alone.

On the weekends and when school was out, Clasteen and I would sometimes make dolls out of cloth scraps that our mother would give us. Like me, she had an active imagination, so together, we made a doll house using cardboard boxes we'd found and we'd make up voices for the dolls and create adventures for them.

Eight year-old Margaret on the farm.

3

During the hours Clasteen was in school and was still too young to tell time, I would mark the day by the regular occurrences in my world.

Midday was when the farm bell rang signaling to the farmers that it was time to check in for lunch, and most of the time, this was also the time my dad would find a switch and drive to the elementary school to question what my brother Kenneth had done to disrupt the educational process.

One time, Kenneth got angry and threw a round piece of jagged tin at another student. Fortunately he missed. Another time, he snuck under the teacher's desk and pulled her stockings. He was smart – maybe the smartest of the Bynum children - but he was also full of nervous energy and always in trouble for something.

So whenever I heard the bell, I'd always run as fast I could to my father's car and wait there so maybe I could go with him. Once he'd finished up conferring with Kenneth's teacher and likely whipping my brother, we'd go back to the farm for lunch. I loved the ride into town and the time alone with my daddy.

He was never a talkative man, but he was fair and honest and he didn't have to say a lot for me to know he loved me.

After lunch, my dad would return to the field to continue with his work and I would go back to playing in the yard by myself or with the dogs. I was always hoping something interesting would happen. Of course, when nothing did, I would do my best to create something interesting. Some of those times reminded me Kenneth wasn't the only one to get into trouble.

As the daughter of a sharecropper, we had many chores. I was designated as the one to baby-sit my younger brother, Raymond, who should not have existed.

Once Raymond and I were playing leap frog and he wanted me to jump over him but I said no because I was too big. But he insisted so I tried, but I bumped him and he hit his head on the hardwood floor causing a knot as big as a baseball. This must have scared my parents something awful because I got whipped so badly after all these years, I still can vividly feel the pain.

Another time, Raymond and I were playing and I told him to

climb up on the dresser and jump off so I could catch him. I don't know why I said that because I had no intention of catching him, so when he jumped, I pulled back my arms and he hit the floor with a thud. I suppose I probably got whipped pretty badly for that, as well, but I don't remember.

My most memorable time as a sitter, however, revolved around a mean old rooster.

That crotchety animal had bothered me pretty much since the first time I saw it. It had beady eyes and an ugly disposition and would always chase me and try and peck at me, so one day, I decided to teach it a lesson. My plan was to go into the yard with Raymond and when the rooster advanced, I'd whack it with the broom and then run into the house with my little brother. My parents and siblings had all gone to work in the fields picking cotton and the two of us were left alone so this seemed like the perfect time.

Well, part of the plan materialized when I swung the broom in hopes of frightening the rooster. But when I missed and the rooster started chasing me, I became scared realizing the door had locked and now we had no place to hide. All I could do was build a sort of barricade and hope for the best.

So for the hours until the family returned, Raymond and I sought refuge between the locked door and the screen door. Until then, the mean and patient rooster just pecked away at items on the ground never giving us enough space to escape. We both cried and cried until my family got close enough to the house to hear and rescue us.

Of course, there were fun times, too.

On Sundays, we children played dodge ball, baseball, and hide and seek. Sometimes, Clasteen and I would climb trees as high as we could and then race back down to the bottom. She was always faster than me because she had longer legs, but I didn't care; it was just fun to play.

One of my other favorite games was cowboys-and-crooks.

5

We'd chase each other around the year, good guys trying to capture bad guys and vice versa. Those we captured got tied up, of course, and one time I got cornered and tied up and my brothers and sisters put me up on the roof of the house where the only way down was to jump. I don't remember having a cast on my arms or legs, so I guess I made it down okay.

Getting hurt wasn't really a consideration for kids aiming to have a good time. We would climb inside an old tire and someone would roll us as fast as they could until we fell. We swatted bumblebees with a flat bat, but had to run fast if we missed so we wouldn't get stung by the angry bees. I still have a scar on my chest from running with a stick nailed to a can. The can hit a rock and stopped but I didn't.

City children don't get to play the way we did. And children growing up in families with money got toys and games, so they didn't need to be so creative with their entertainment. As I think about it, I believe we were lucky to have the opportunity to live in a world that inspired creativity. I doubt I'd want to change those days at all, even if I had the opportunity.

Momma's name was Sophia but we all, except my baby brother, called her Soph.

She was tall for a woman in those days, probably 5'7", and although not fat, she was also not frail, as many tall women are. She had a dress on every day, even when she was working around the house or alongside Daddy in the fields, and she always wore glasses with brown rims which served to accentuate her plain face and severe nature.

Daddy's name was Roosevelt, but people – including us kids - called him Velts. He was considerably shorter in stature than Momma, and thinner, too, maybe 120 pounds soaking wet. Daddy would wear bib overalls and a button down cap nearly every day. I always knew his was a weekend alcoholic with a preference for the moonshine, but it wasn't something we talked about out loud.

While Daddy took care of Kenny's disciplining, Momma handled Clasteen and me by administering the punishment. She would give us a look that said that was the end of that, and we'd quickly comply because she was not the type of person you wanted to disappoint.

Like many people in the south, my parents had grown up part of small family churches that held services once a month. The other Sundays, we would visit other churches that were close by.

One day, my parents decided Clasteen and I were of an age to be baptized so the pastor or the church arranged for this to occur in the river that ran through Handsome, a small community near Newsome.

But the thought of wading into that muddy water with who knows what slimy thing lining its murky bed, and who knows how many angry fish ready to nip at our feet, was a supremely unpleasant concept. So on the day of our baptism, Clasteen and I walked slowly with our heads down as if we were headed not to a spiritual rebirth, but to the gallows.

It was a sunny day and there were a number of fishermen out along the banks. My brother Kenneth and a couple of my male cousins ran on ahead to where a little boat was tied up. None of them could swim well, and Kenneth was taunting the other boys, trying to goad them into climbing into the boat and floating out a ways.

Boys being boys, one of them complied. Unfortunately, that one was my first cousin on my Momma's side, Steve Willis, who was about 14 or 15 and was wearing his best suit.

Kenneth may have thought the boat was tied to a stump, or maybe not, but when it started floating out too far and Steve realized he had no oars to get back, he jumped into the water wearing that nice suit.

Kenneth got a whipping right then and there. And perhaps the commotion scared the fish to another part of the lake because Clasteen and I got baptized without a single nip.

Our home was better than a shack but less than modest, even by Newsome standards.

There was a front room parlor, a dining room and a kitchen. Momma and Daddy had a bedroom, and there were two more bedrooms: one for the girls and one for the boys, each with one big bed.

Being the youngest, I slept between my two older sisters, always being too cold if one disliked the covers or too hot when both decided to stay covered; always silently seething at the lack of control over something as basic as my own comfort.

As we grew, we were given more chores to help around the house.

Because we had no electricity, Clasteen and I had to use paper from the Sears catalog to clean the lamp glass because it got all sooty from the burning kerosene. For cooking and heat, we children gathered wood from the forest and brought it to Momma who kept it stored on the porch near the kitchen.

No electricity meant no refrigeration, so the ice man - who came by on horse-draw-wagon or truck - brought our ice which we kept in a big square ice box in the back. We also had no indoor plumbing, so we had to bring in water from the pump or the well to use for washing, and use the outhouse located back behind our main house. I honestly didn't think of any of this as being unusual, but it sometimes brought challenges.

Perhaps I should restate that. I say I didn't think of it as being unusual, but that did not mean I liked it.

It was experiences like this that kept us from ever using the outhouse at night. Instead, we had a bucket that we called a slop jar that was kept in the house; but Momma would get angry if someone had to use it. Another thing we did without was toilet paper the way it is packaged today. Like other farm folks, we used the pages from the big catalogs that came in the mailbox. It was just another thing I took for granted, but once again, that didn't mean I liked it.

On the farm, we had chickens. They were mean and would chase me across the yard, but they had a purpose as we swapped their eggs for milk from a neighbor who had a cow. I liked eggs as a child. Momma would crack them into melted cheese which was delicious. But one time Clasteen and I were in the hayloft getting a few for Momma and we found one that was rotten. It had an awful smell which turned my stomach almost immediately. Clasteen thought that was very funny and, thereafter, when she wanted some of my food she'd say 'Remember the loft' and I would feel sick and she'd get my food. I seldom eat eggs to this day.

The majority of the farmland was dedicated to growing peanuts, corn, and cotton. We picked them all, too. When it was time to harvest the cotton, there was a strategy we always followed which was to pick two rows a day. I remember Momma would fix breakfast and then we'd begin the picking. When everyone had worked his or her way to the end of the row, it was time for lunch. And it was the same thing after lunch until supper time.

The land owner was named Dick Darden. My Daddy used to say he took money from us. I don't know if that was true, but I do know we worked an awful lot without ever getting rich from the effort.

— —

Like many men in those days, chewing tobacco was common. I thought it was very cool and became interested in trying it for myself. I suppose you know how this will turn out, but I may as well give you the details so that, should you never have tried tobacco, you may be spared the experience.

Momma's brother had some tobacco and left it in the house when he went to help in the fields. Clasteen and I were in the house along and found that clump of tobacco and figured this was the perfect time to give it a try.

We were unsure as to whether we were supposed to just

chew it or swallow it, so we chewed for a while, then went on to swallow. The taste was bad, but the way it made us feel was worse. Worse still has having to go into the field to find Momma and tell her what we had done.

Years later, when I tried to smoke, I got violently sick. I believe this experience was probably why.

Tobacco wasn't the only vice available out in the country. My parents used to make wine from grapes and peaches. We children would help by taking pots and filling them with water, and they'd add the fermented fruit and the other ingredients.

After the tobacco experience, though, I was about done with trying things meant for people older than me.

On Thursday nights, we'd always go over to my uncle's house.

We would get there in time for Kraft Playhouse 90, then the men would watch the boxing matches which were presented by Schlitz and Pabst Blue Ribbon beers. That was back when beer companies could have television commercials and Joe Lewis, Jersey Joe Wolcott, and Rocky Graziano were the popular fighters. These were tough men, and my Daddy and his brother and all would drink while they were watching them fight, each yelling at the television as if he had a stake in the results.

Momma used to go to my uncle's house to watch television, too. But it was during the day and instead of watching the fights, she and my aunt and some other ladies would watch the soap operas and the news. How I hated those hours.

Whatever we'd be doing – even if it was working in the field – we'd have to come in and wash out faces and feet and get ready to go with her. Then we'd have to sit quietly while the ladies watched so as not to distract them from the story line. Each soap was fifteen minutes: Love of Life, then Search for Tomorrow, then the news, and then The Guiding Light. Adults fighting, dramas, and love stories weren't to my liking: they made me feel tense and I felt they were way too serious for no reason.

I still hate soap operas.

I was 12 and in high school when we finally did get electricity.

As I remember, the local electric company put in the wiring for the electricity. When they got finished, I remember thinking it didn't look like the other places I'd been where there was electricity. For instance, the big tangled bundles of wires slung up near the ceiling throughout the house. At night, I would lay in my bed looking up at them, worrying what would happen if they fell on me and my sisters, or my little brother down the hall.

I worried a lot in those days. Mostly about what other people thought of me.

Clasteen, who had always been a pretty, athletic child, had grown into a lithe, graceful young woman. Her hair was jet black and shiny,

Margaret in her teens.

falling to her shoulders in a style called a Pageboy. Her hands were thin and her fingers long to play the piano. She was smart, and clever, and well-liked at school. I wanted to be like her so much, I can still feel the dull ache of the low self-esteem that characterized my childhood.

My own hair wouldn't grow, so Momma always made me wear it cropped close to my head or in cornrows. And my arms and legs were chubby rendering me unable to excel at even the simplest of sports. I was pudgy all over and always one of the shortest in my class. I'd ask to borrow Clasteen's clothes, but she'd always turn me down because I was too big. But the shoes were the worst thing.

Clasteen wouldn't let me wear her shoes, and neither would my older sister because although their size was the same as mine, they said I'd wear them out with my flat-footed gait and the extra weight I would place on them.

They were so ladylike and I was just a chubby baby sister.

———

When Clasteen practiced the piano, she'd lock the door. I used to sit there on the other side squinting into the keyhole so I could watch her. I wanted to play the piano, too, so I enrolled in a music class in high school, thinking I would have the same talent as my sister. We had cardboard piano keys that we placed on our desk. But I was so bad that the teacher would hit my knuckles with a ruler which, as you might expect, made practicing rather difficult, so after a while I just gave up trying to play piano like Clasteen.

Studying was a similar challenge. I would study for three days and barely earn a passing grade. Clasteen would barely open her book and easily ace a test.

I guess it was my jealousy that caused us to fight all the time. Sometimes, we'd just look at each other and start fighting. Other times, because her skin was darker than mine, I would call her "Black" which she didn't like. But it was the only ammunition I had in my scarce arsenal.

———

Still, I knew Clasteen loved me. For the most part, I knew that because of how she would protect me at school.

Being smallish, and roundish, and quiet, I was an easy target for bullies. But every day after school, Clasteen would ask me if anyone had said or done anything to upset me that day, and if someone had, she'd take care of them after school, on the way home. I felt safe as long as I knew she was in my corner.

— ◆ —

Another highlight of my high school years was my friend Quinis. She was a quiet girl, like me, but she was always pleasant to be around. So much so that I didn't even mind that – like Clasteen – she was tall and thin. We would talk about typical school things, events, teachers, and class assignments. Unlike a lot of high school girls, we didn't talk much about boys. But that was okay with me. Other than my brothers, they were a mystery I was not at an emotional place to begin to solve.

In 1952, we got our own television, so, thankfully, we no longer had to go to my uncle's to watch soap operas. It was the day of Queen Elizabeth's inauguration and I can still clearly remember how impressed I was with the pomp and circumstance of it all. Her back was straight and her clothing looked like nothing in even most expensive catalogs we received. I watched her and thought of all the things someone like that must know that I would never even begin to think of. But it was on all three of the channels we could get and I remember being so upset because for that whole entire day, it was the only thing available for us to watch.

Television back then ran from 6 a.m. to 10 p.m. and ended with the Star Spangled Banner. I would watch anytime I could. I especially liked the cartoons on Saturday. And I'd always rush home from school to see Gabby Hayes and American Band Stand.

Sometimes, we'd all go to the community center where my Daddy liked to play baseball. Lots of people would be there, and Clasteen and I could go to the center building where there was a juke box so we could listen to the music and Clasteen would dance.

— ◆ —

It took only one year for the wiring to start a fire.

Momma was near home when she saw the flames. She started screaming to alert anyone within earshot. Everyone who could came running to help, but although they did their best, it was too late. We lost everything except Raymond's guitar and the electric stove my dad had won at a department store grand opening.

As devastating as it was to lose most of our belongings, the fire meant we were free to move into town. After all, the land owner was unlikely to rebuild something our faulty wiring had destroyed.

I comforted myself with the knowledge that no more would we have to plant and harvest every weekend and all through the holidays. No more would we have to feed the pigs and mules and ducks and geese and dogs and cats. Life was surely about to change and my own life was about to change in a big way.

My parents built us a new house in the next largest city, Franklin.

Thinking back, though, it hardly seems correct to call it a city as there were only about 2,700 people there, but it seemed powerfully large compared with Newsome's few people.

In Franklin, the homes were placed closer together than the farm homes were. And there were stores we could walk to without going far. Best in my estimation, of course, was that we had better wiring, so less chance of another fire.

I had been to Franklin before we moved there. Back when we lived on the farm, my parents would go to Franklin on Saturdays. It was my Momma's only day out of the house and I have little doubt she looked forward to it each week.

I didn't much look forward to those days, though, and this was because my siblings would use the time to get into trouble doing one thing or another they knew they were not supposed to do. Then when my parents returned, they'd ask us what's we'd been up to and try as I might, I found it difficult to tell a fib while looking at that leather belt and/or switch that they used to punish us.

One time, one or my two oldest brothers decided the hay loft full of corn out in the barn was a possible source of riches for him, so he took a mule cart full into Newsome to sell it. I guess he thought that since he'd helped to harvest it, that corn was rightfully his, but I don't think my parents agreed, and when they got word of this bit of risky business, they confronted us kids.

"Which one of you took the corn?" they asked.

No one said anything. But then Momma stared right at me as if she could see right into my brain and I got so nervous, I began to cry which led to my tattling on my brothers.

This type of event would often result in at least the instigator getting a whipping. And as a result, my siblings – particularly those with instigator tendencies – would gang up on me when Momma and Daddy were gone, so my parents got into the habit of taking me with them to keep me safe and sound.

Today, I'd call that a win-win. Then, I simply considered it an opportunity to escape harm and see the city with my parents. So when we eventually moved there, I was already somewhat familiar with the place.

Mind you, in our Franklin home we still didn't have indoor toilets, and a water pump attached to our porch provided water. But still, life was different in the city. And different was good. For one thing, it taught me the concepts of perspective and culture.

I remember the first visit to my friend's home on a Sunday afternoon where they were having fried chicken for lunch. That was unheard of in my family because we only ate fried foods for breakfast and other two meals included baked or boiled meats. And here they were, seemingly normal people enjoying a fried lunch!

I wondered if that was a city custom that we would soon be adopting to better fit in or if we would stay the same. And

I thought we'd likely not make the change too quickly because there were so many other things that required adaptation.

For instance, the grocery stores were, to me, enormous, and my parents had to spend at least $10 each time they went there. Quite a difference from our lives on the farm where we made or traded with other nearby families for most everything we needed.

On the farm, we grew our own vegetables and raised hogs and chickens. Even though we didn't have a cow of our own, one of our neighbors did and we got milk from them. We even made soap from the hog fat. We only purchased a few things from the general store, such as cheese, and molasses, and flour for making bread.

Even some of our clothes were what today we'd consider vintage recycled (and probably tie a hefty price to). What I'm speaking of are the flour sack dresses Momma would make Clasteen and me.

You think of such a thing now and it makes you laugh. But back then, choosing the color or pattern on the sack was often cause for argument between Clasteen and I, just as any two girls faced with a single choice in dress style would experience.

No more.

Now we went to the store for what we needed.

Momma said it was the way things were done when you lived in the city and we knew better than to argue with Momma.

Sometimes, I'd get sent to the store for things, but I'd always seem to get interested in something I saw along the way and lose track of time. I remember so many times realizing I was late and running home as fast as I could, but always taking too long.

Another city change came from our proximity to others and the independence that an enterprising girl like me, who was used to farm labor, might find if she applied herself. Specifically, since we no longer lived on the farm, we could work for others; a desirable concept because it meant that although I would be expected to contribute to the family accounts, I could also make some money of my own. Needless to say, I sought work opportunities whenever and wherever I could.

One day Clasteen and I asked if we could skip school. I had seen a sign advertising for people to pick strawberries and thought that seemed like an excellent fit as we had both field experience and a love of the fruit. We were to be paid by the five cents for each tray, so I was excited when the bus picked us up early in the morning knowing I could get in a full day. And I did. About ten hours' worth.

Problem was that for every strawberry I put in the basket, I probably put two in my mouth. So needless to say, when the day was over, I had a belly ache from the strawberries and just 95 cents in my pocket.

On another occasion, my friend and classmate, Quinis invited me to go on a farm trip where we would pull cabbage plants. She was under the impression that we would make a $1 for every hundred plants. Like me, she longed for the independence that some cash provided, so we were always scheming for ways we could make a few dollars.

This was unheard of money in those days and we figured working together, we could easily move several hundred plants in short order.

We got up early to make sure there was space on the back of the truck for us. We were excited knowing this would be the most money we would have earned so far. But when we got there, and were given our instructions for the day, we found the man planned on paying a dollar for every *thousand* plants, not every hundred.

We were given large buckets for the plants. My friend pulled the plants, but I just sat underneath a tree in the shade and watched her. I would have left, but I did not have a way to get home until the end of the day, I went home without earning any money. We called that the end of our time as field hands.

My next job was a paper route carrier where I earned ten cents for every newspaper that I sold. It, too, seemed like an excellent opportunity for a friendly and motivated girl, but they only sent me about 20 papers a week, so the most I could make for my efforts was $2.00 which quickly ended my newspaper career.

➤ ━

You know, all the time I was living on the farm and for much of my first months in the city, I never knew we were what you'd call poor. As far as my perspective allowed, we were a normal family with all the day-to-day joys and woes that make up this life.

There were relatives coming and going most all the time and some may have had more than us in terms of material things, but not so much more that you would notice it.

We'd go to see relatives, too. One of my favorite times was Easter Monday which both a day off of school and a large family celebration. We would go to a nearby cousin's house and have a huge Easter egg hunt. There would be homemade ice cream and we children would eat lunch while the adults hid the eggs, then we would search for the eggs, then play all day. I looked forward to that day all year.

I have vague recollections of my paternal grandmother and maternal grandfather who lived with us for a short time when my Momma was ill. My grandfather was an oddly quiet man. He was short, I suppose, but, of course, he was taller than me. I can picture him sitting at the table, but I cannot remember the sound of his voice or a single conversation we may have had. I have better recollections of my grandmother Martha, especially the time she gave Kenneth a whipping.

It was 1945 and we were sitting in my dad's old car which was a Model T, I think. The car was only used to go to the general store in town and to church. We walked everywhere else. But Kenneth, who had in no way mellowed, cared only about playing tricks and having fun. That day, he did something to upset our grandmother but all I could remember was that Clasteen and I watched as he was punished once again. No one got hurt in the car, but Kenneth did find a few extra bumps when Grandmother Martha got finished with him.

Kenneth was, as I've said, a difficult young man. When he disappeared a few years later, and after he had graduated from Hayden High School, I don't think it came as a surprise to anyone in our family. What was surprising is that he came home in the uniform of an Air Force serviceman.

When we asked why he chose to join the service, he said he was always interested in flight, adding the story of when he'd been in high school and asked his science teacher a question.

"How long do you think it will be before man walks on the moon?" he asked.

The teacher responded, "Three days of detention for asking such a dumb question."

I don't remember much about my grandparents so this information was obtained from my brother, Linwood, and my

Kenneth graduated and joined the Air Force.

cousin, Randolph. My grandmother lived to be 75, much of those last years as a widow as her husband, my grandfather Randall, only lived a little past 60. She was representative of most of the women in my family on my dad's side who also had long lives. My great-grandmother, Ida Murray, lived to be the grand old age of 110.

My dad's brothers were all farmers and stayed in the South. His sisters all moved to New Jersey. My dad was not the favorite brother so the sisters and their families, even though they visited the South every year, would drive by our house but would not stop. If we were to see them, we had to visit at my uncle's house. Soon my mom got tired of that, so we stopped visiting. My uncles all had lots of children except for one. Two had in excess of twelve children and the one uncle had three. He was the youngest and the favorite. He also had a better car and house than the others. Now, as I look back, I'm sure it was because my uncle had more space for visitors to stay.

To my knowledge, Charlie Peete, my cousin and brother to Randolph, was the only famous member of our family. But sadly, his fame was short-lived. Always an athlete, Charlie especially liked baseball. He became a professional baseball player for the St. Louis Cardinals. He was excited about going to Venezuela to train, and insistent that his family accompany him on this adventure. No one really knew exactly what happened or why he decided to take a separate flight from the rest of the team so he could travel with his family, but the plane on which they were travelling crashed, killing all of them.

My memory will never erase the image of those five white caskets lined up at the front of the church, and the palpable grief of the people filing in for the funeral services. Charlie Peete, his wife, and his three pretty little daughters would always remain in our hearts in spirit.

My mother's family lived in Handsome, Virginia on the Bryant Plantation. My mother had one sister, who died at the age of 18, and four brothers: John, Leroy, Willie, and Pompy.

Many years later, while serving as Principal at San Andreas High School, I was fortunate enough to take the Underground Railroad. I believe it was 2001 or 2002. It was an awesome experience traveling from San Bernardino to Cincinnati, Ohio, then to Kentucky, Michigan and then to Canada where those enslaved were freed. I had a chance to visit Harriet Beecher Stowe's home, the cemetery where the Wright Brothers and Paul Lawrence Dunbar are buried, the original Uncle Tom's Cabin, and a few homes that were safe homes for the slaves. The greatest experience was being right there in a holding place for slaves where so many had stayed as part of their journey to freedom

On that trip, while visiting the Hamilton County Library Archives, I located many Bynum's who were listed as slaves and lived in North Carolina I had seven great aunts: Henrietta, Laura, Annie, Dora, Lucy, Molly, and Martha, and a great uncle, Louis Murray, on my dad's side of the family. And I had four paternal aunts: Henrietta, Annie, Mae, and Esther, and three paternal uncles: James, Randall, and Glynnis.

The awesome responsibility in honoring their lives became a mission over time. But more about that later on.

One of my relatives, we called him Uncle Ryland, was very light skinned with naturally curly hair. He lived in Mt. Vernon, New York and would visit us once a year during the summer. I often wondered how he got in the family with those features, so when John Lee, my first cousin on my mother's side, told me about the Bryant Plantation, I understood.

One of Uncle Ryland's sons, Kenneth, visited us once during the summer /vacation. He was a young teenager, very handsome and very articulate and always acted as if he knew more than we did and so he needed to teach us something. Even with that attitude, I looked forward to his visit since no one ever visited us for a period of time.

Hunt Elementary School.

One evening, my brother, Buddy (who, as you remember, was *also* named Kenneth), was standing on the back porch of my parent's home with the rest of us when my city cousin, Kenneth, decided to show us how a hangman's noose worked.

I don't know what possessed him to do such a thing – maybe he was just showing off by demonstrating he knew how to do something we did not – but he tied that knot, then stood up on one of our porch chairs to throw the end over an eave, then slipped the noose over his own head and tightened it. He was laughing and pretending to strangle, so I guess Buddy thought he'd help him be more realistic and he kicked the chair away, causing my cousin to dangle.

Buddy laughed at him. But the rest of us all just stood there frozen in shock as he gasped for air, struggling to pull the rope away from his neck. He probably would have died had my mother not heard the commotion and rushed out to put the chair down below his feet.

I attended a two-room schoolhouse, Hunt Elementary, from grades one through seven. We walked and shared stories on the way to and from school each day. The schools were segregated then and the white students got to take a bus while we had to walk, but often we'd stop and talk to them as they waited. Our conversations were polite and good natured, as most conversations between children are. We'd share what has happening at our respective schools and then their bus would arrive, and we'd go back to walking to our school.

With elementary school teacher Mrs. Baker-Holman.

We'd heard our parents talking about segregation and we saw things in the news, but we shared the commonality of youth and were friendly and respectful of each other. We didn't question why we attended different schools; we simply accepted the fact that schools were segregated institutions.

I had begun school at the age of five only because my father was the cook and the gardener for the school in addition to the work he did on the farm. My birthday came in December which meant I was supposed to start school the following school year, but since Daddy was there, it made sense for me to just go with him.

While it may have been a convenience for my father, early attendance was a detriment to a little girl who was not prepared to sit still in the classroom or complete her lessons. These simply weren't things I'd considered before.

My first teacher, Miss Joann Baker, was in charge of grades one through three and all the students were educated in one classroom. She was young and very attractive but I felt she just didn't like me and it was probably because I was not a good student and somewhat lazy. If we didn't do our homework, we had to line up, hold out our hand and get our ten swats with the ruler. My hand was usually sore.

It may also have been because Miss Baker had taught my older sister Clasteen, who, as I have said, had great academic abilities. Clasteen never took the time to show me how to do better, but she always made it a point to laugh at me for my inability to do well in school.

When I got to the next teacher, who taught grades four through seven in the other classroom, things did not get much better.

Mrs. Estelle Brown was an older woman, but was very pleasant and seemed to like me more than my first teacher. She was quiet, short of stature, and had small, delicate features. Her demeanor was nurturing and very compassionate, even to a struggling student like myself.

I knew Mrs. Brown cared about me, but it didn't make me a better student. So even after several years getting used to the schedule of the classroom, I continued having a difficult time learning and school remained a challenge for me.

I guess Clasteen had given up on hoping her Babysis would ever be the student she was, but she did lend a hand when I was bullied by other students. She would approach me at the end of the school day and ask, "Who bothered you today?" I would give her the name and the fight was on.

This protection ended when Clasteen went on to high school, which began with the 8th grade. You would think that a child who was not academically inclined would probably know how to protect herself, but that wasn't the case. I spent my entire seventh grade year running home almost daily and very scared to keep from getting in a fight, something I rarely accomplished.

When I finished elementary school, I got the opportunity to ride the bus to the high school that was about twenty miles away in the city of Franklin. It was a thrill thinking of the nice ride to high school, and the socializing I'd be able to do with my friends. But I soon discovered that you had to sit still and be quiet on the bus, thus ending that imagined spree.

Hayden High School graduating class of 1957.

Then after the fire, we were much closer to school, and I could just ride in the car with my mother, which was only on rainy days or walk with Clasteen and her friends. It wasn't like today when children are driven everywhere. We were taught to look both ways and not talk to strangers. Period.

I didn't like school, but staying home would have meant I had to work in the field or do housework, so I chose school. Monday through Friday, from 9 a.m. until 3:30 p.m., we attended Hayden High School, a two-story brick high school for grades eight through eleven.

The teachers at Hayden were very different from those at my previous school. In the first place, there were many more of them. And they each taught a specific subject, so you had to not only learn the subject, but the teacher's expectations for your mastery of that subject.

For a student like me, this posed numerous challenges. And although my parents insisted I read my text books every evening after school, I spent most of that time pretending to read, wasting the possibility of absorbing anything.

The grading system was different than today. We received one credit per class, with 16 credits needed to graduate. You didn't know if you had passed a class until the end of the year and if you failed a single class, you would have to repeat the entire year. Being a borderline student and knowing I was not studying to my parents' standards, I was worried all the time.

It was also strange having a male teacher since I had not even seen one the first seven years of school; they were particularly difficult to understand.

I remember my music teacher because he gave us a senior assignment that was due the day before graduation. It consisted of a 3,000 word report. I wrote what I thought was the required number of words and turned it in, but then the day before graduation, he informed me it was only 2,200 words and, therefore, he could not pass me in the class and I would not graduate the next day. Can you believe that man counted every word? I stayed up the entire night writing the remaining 800 words.

My science teacher would write sentences on the chalkboard in tiny print and we had to fill in the missing word. I could barely read his writing, let alone remember what the missing word was.

→ ←

The shorthand teacher just thought I was stupid and not capable of mastering the subject. I received a failing grade the first reporting period, but I was so fascinated with the symbology of shorthand that I taught myself. By the time I left high school, I was taking dictation at one-hundred words a minute.

The combination of where we lived and my parents' lack of education, I am sure, contributed to some of my difficulties. There is no denying that we were truly Southern Hicks. I remember telling my typing teacher that I wanted to be a secretary someday and her replying that would never happen with my dialect and vocabulary.

There was one teacher, though, who I felt, really liked me, but to this day I cannot remember what she taught. I assumed that she liked me because she always asked if she could take me home on the weekends. We didn't have hot running water at home, so it might have just been to clean me up. But that didn't matter to me. I liked her companionship and the fact that she treated me like someone who might have the capability to contribute to this world in some way.

I may not have realized it at the time, but I learned to be a better person from my teachers. I learned to understand people can be so different, with varying ways of showing they care for you and this doesn't mean you are wrong, or that they are. I think they all wanted me to do my best; I simply didn't understand they were telling me that in a different way from which I'd previously been told.

As I remember, none of my teachers ever called my mom on me and I was never suspended for anything I did, or did not do. Each, in their own way, taught me to be respectful whether I liked what was happening or not, and whether or not I was good at a certain subject. I guess they taught me patience, which is a skill one cannot acquire from a book.

The thing that bothered me the most about high school was the fact that they used alphabetical seating charts which meant I was always in the front of the classroom because my last name began with the letter "B."

Being short in stature also provided no benefit, as I was always in the front of the line when we had to line up for activities.

I tried a few things, but I'm not sure why.

For instance, I joined the Future Business Leaders Association. And I tried out for the choir. There were a lot of students there and we all had to sing "Swing Low, Sweet Chariot." I sang a stanza and then they asked me to sing again, but I never got called back. I was okay, though, because all the time I was trying out, I knew I couldn't sing well.

I also tried cheating on a test once.

It was for tenth grade Civics class, which was an odd choice as I actually had been doing well in Civics. But I had seen other students cheat and they said how easy it was to do. So the day of the test, I went into class with notes written on a tiny sheet of paper that I tried – and failed – to hide in my hand.

My teacher, Miss Smith, asked, "Are those notes in your hand, Margaret Bynum?"

"Yes, ma'am," I said.

I flunked the test.

And, I remained in the shadow of my sister, Clasteen.

She had been a good student in elementary school, but by high school

My Sister Clasteen in High School.

had blossomed into a brilliant and skilled young woman. She could dance and sing like a professional. She could outplay anyone on the basketball court. And her shiny long hair and beautiful white teeth that made her look like a teen angel naturally drew people to her.

I, on the other hand, had not developed talents for dancing or singing. I had not developed athletic ability at all. And my hair was thin and dull and usually worn in braids/corn rows. I had few friends, and, other than by our last name, it would have been difficult for people to know we were sisters at all.

I guess maybe someone wanted to make a joke when, in the Hayden High School Olympics, I represented the seniors in the fifty-yard dash. I don't think anyone was either surprised or disappointed when I came in last place.

I didn't go to the prom. I didn't even tell my mom there was a prom.

But I remember her coming back from town and saying someone had asked her if I was going, which is how she found out.

Fact was, I was as scared of boys as I was of most things. Once, a fellow asked if he could hold my hand as we walked home from school and I was petrified. I was so naïve then, I used to think if a boy looked at you, you'd get pregnant, and I sure didn't want to ever have that happen.

Mostly, that was as a result of Clasteen's personal mistake of getting pregnant when she was 16.

We never talked about it much, and I don't remember Momma and Daddy having a talk with the boy's parents, but I do remember that Momma made me sit outside the bedroom where Clasteen was giving birth on that hot Saturday morning. She was screaming in pain and Momma was telling me that if I didn't want to suffer the same fate, I would stay far away from boys.

That could well be why I never had children of my own.

I graduated in 1957 at age 16 as an eleventh grader. There was no 12th grade in high school until 1959.

Now that I think about it, I was ready to leave home as soon as I hit my senior year, and did not have plans of returning except to visit my family. As a matter of fact, I attended the high school reunion twenty-five years later and nothing had changed. There were one or two class-mates there who remembered me and the ones who were popular in high school still ran the show.

It was odd, then, when I went back for my fiftieth reunion and was amazed at the number of people who remembered me. As a matter of fact, I paid for my baby brother and his wife to go with me because, as much as I wanted to attend, I didn't want to sit all alone. They were as surprised as I. I was more popular at the

My graduation photo.

reunion than I was in high school and believe it or not, more people remembered me than I expected.

CHAPTER TWO

How to Graduate College in Seven Years

The greatest gift may not be respect, but it's in the top ten.
~Margaret Hill

I left home to start college in August of 1957. I was 16 years old, moving from Franklin's population of 2,700 people 60 miles away to Norfolk, Virginia, a Navy town with a population of 350,000.

If I had felt socially inadequate at Hayden High School, it was nothing compared to the culture shock I felt so far from the life I had known. I missed the comfort of knowing what was around each corner. Many weekends, I'd go home to see my family, and, as my mother had decided with five of the six children now out on their own the family should own a telephone, I could also call. I may have been unprepared for my expanding life, but at the same time, I felt a level of exhilaration I had not previously known.

Norfolk State College – now called Norfolk State University and listed as one of the Historical Black Colleges – was a small, all-Black school in Virginia. My mother insisted I attend Norfolk State. She knew I was a speedy typist and could do shorthand at about one hundred words a minute when I left high school, and she felt those skills combined with a degree would guarantee me a good secretarial job someday. I was to major in secretarial science and complete the program in two years.

Of course, I said, "No way."

I respected my mother, but I also had listened to my teachers who I felt were most in tune with my academic abilities. Most all of them had done an excellent job of assuring me that I would not make it in college and that I should seek employment in one of the local factories. They had witnessed my poor grammar and average grades before making the assessment about what my career plans should be

But in those days, parents always won the battle, so on to Norfolk I went.

I had thought to major in Accounting and filled out my applications to that end, but changed my major to Business Education with a minor in English before the ink dried. I still think of this as ironic because I believe that I have always been a substandard English speaker.

There were no dormitories at the school, so my mother found me a room at an Opportunity Home where I did the washing, ironing, general cleaning and babysitting for a family of four. This two-story house was beautiful and included four bedrooms. Even so, I still had to share a bedroom with their young daughter.

I did not have the time to participate in extracurricular activities because I had to report to the home as soon as school was out so that I could do my chores and still have time for homework, but I was interested in becoming a member of the drill team. Unfortunately, my opportunity home family did not feel I should take time away from them to participate in this activity.

I am usually not strong willed; however, being in the drill team was one of the things I truly wanted to do. Happily, they eventually gave in and allowed me to participate.

There were, however, areas in which we did not come to such an amicable agreement. For instance, we did not agree on having a dog in the house. I suppose this is mostly because I would be the one assigned to clean up after it.

One night, the dog had an accident. I saw this had happened when I was on my way to school the next morning, but I was dressed and clean and simply didn't want to touch that mess, nor did I want to be late to my first class, so I just left.

When I got home, I knew I was in trouble. It did not help when I was asked, "What should you do when you get up in the morning and there is dog waste on the floor?" and I responded, "It would not happen to me because I would never keep a dog in the house."

I left in December of 1957 when I went home for Christmas break. It was then that the news came that I would need to find another place to live.

I wasn't terribly upset.

━▶ ◀━

I spent my second semester in a home that was owned by a minister who lived in one of the rooms, rented the downstairs to a Navy family and the remainder of the upstairs to three of us girls.

The family was made up of the parents and four kids. The husband was the cook on a ship and he also cooked many of the meals at home, which was a wonderful treat for us, as the family would eat on Sunday at about three to four o'clock and then let us girls have the leftovers. That meant we didn't have to buy food that day, and the food they provided was home-cooked and very delicious.

But one day, the girls and I had gone into town to shop and we returned at five o'clock to find a full kitchen full of prepared food. Thinking the family had decided to go out, we ate nearly every bit of it. They family got back shortly after – unfortunately for us - expecting to have the meal they had left, and found it gone.

We felt awful, of course.

It was just a misunderstanding, but I learned to always ask first and not take things for granted. Even now when I am at home, I ask my husband, Bob, if he wants any more of whatever we have made before I finish it.

When school started for my second year of college, I was without a place to stay and my mother suggested that I move in with a cousin, actually my mother's cousin, a much older woman. She was part Indian but somewhat eccentric, I thought. When my friends came to see me and *if* she answered the doorbell, she began teaching them.

"I came by to see Margaret," one might say.

"Don't you think you should ask me how I am doing?" she would reply.

"Sure. Is Margaret in?" my friend would ask.

"Who are your parents? I will only allow people with influential parents to enter my home," the landlady would retort.

"Tell Margaret that I will see her at school tomorrow," my friend would say before my landlady slammed the door.

Needless to say, my visiting friends came to a halt.

I had found a job by perusing the telephone book looking for a job as a shampoo girl in a beauty parlor. That was the only skill I had at that time. You see, my sister and I would take care of each other's hair. I found two wonderful women who gave me an opportunity to work Friday after school and all day Saturday.

One Saturday while working at the salon, I shared a bit about my poor relationship with my cousin. I told the operators that I was miserable there and that I was not allowed to have friends. I even shared that I thought my cousin was crazy and we all laughed. But when I showed up at breakfast the next morning, my cousin and I had the strangest conversation.

"How are you this morning?" my cousin asked.

"I'm fine. What about you?"

"Well, even though I am crazy, I still fixed your breakfast."

"I have a lot of studying to do today," I said.

"Even though I am crazy, I'll make sure that you're not disturbed," she said.

I thought the conversation odd, and then she asked, "Why would you allow the people you work with talk about me?"

"What are you talking about? I asked."

"When you talk about people in a beauty salon, you need to know who's in there," she said. Then I realized someone must have told her what I'd said about her the previous day.

"I know I said things that I should not have said, but who do you know that heard me?" I asked.

"Look out the window," she replied.

I saw the neighbor that I did not know and she had delivered my message. I had to pack again and this time I rented a room from a stranger.

The school year had ended and I didn't want to go home, so I rented a room from the uncle and aunt of a classmate just for a few weeks.

Mr. and Mrs. Johnson were wonderful people who welcomed me into their home with open arms. They prepared my meals and soon learned I enjoyed eating – something I'd struggled with up to that point. I remember one morning at breakfast, Mr. Johnson looked at my sparsely-covered plate and shook his head. He filled my plate, all the while teasing me about weighing an unheard of 125 pounds by the time I turned twenty-five. I was seventeen or eighteen at that time and told him that I would never weigh 125 pounds in my life.

I'm sure he has turned over in his grave about that statement many times.

―――▶ ◀―――

I have learned to build on every experience I have had.

As a matter of fact, I can't think of anything in my life that wasn't in some way a lesson. I have been able to pull some good out of anything, to make lemonade out of lemons. I've had to do it all my life.

It may seem to you that I moved around a lot, generally as a result of my own self-induced misfortunes, and I guess you'd be right in that assumption. My next college residence served as yet another example.

Another high school friend and I found a room at the home of an older lady and her mother who was in her nineties. As the older woman needed her sleep, we couldn't come in late or have company, but we had a roof over our heads, and we had each other for company.

When we got paid, we'd go to the Giant Open Air Market - a retailer that stayed over 24 hours a day and was not too far from the house - to get treats and canned goods for the week. We both worked at the drive-in restaurant and got off work at midnight. One evening, we were at the market talking and laughing and before we knew it, we realized we had to be careful entering the house since we had been warned about entering and disturbing after the women had gone to sleep. We got home very late, later than usual, then tiptoed into the house as quietly as we could being careful not to turn on any lights, but my roommate tripped over some furniture that had been moved earlier that evening while we were gone and I was right behind her. As we fell, we dropped the soda and canned food cans we were carrying and they made a horrible ruckus rolling around the floor waking both ladies. We were asked to leave the following day.

Private homes simply were not working out well for me. So my sixth college residence was at the YWCA which was located just across from the university.

We had to be checked in for the evening by 10 p.m., Sunday through Thursday and 11 p.m. on Friday and Saturday during the school year, but during the summer, we could stay out as late as we wanted to seven days a week. Still, the high school students nearby made fun of us for our mandatory early hours and would tease us when we left whatever establishment we were at when we left. To avoid this, we got creative by obeying our curfew then creeping down the fire escapes, or hanging sheets from the windows to sneak out.

In a nearby city, Virginia Beach, there was a place called Lil's Grill. Once when I was 18, some girlfriends from the Y and I visited this facility courtesy of one of their boyfriends who had a car. While there, listening to the music and chatting together, we met some sailors who were very friendly. We had a fun evening talking and sipping our Cokes and when it got later, my room-mate's boyfriend asked if we were ready to return to the YWCA.

But we really weren't. Instead, we wanted to go to a house party that the military men had invited us to and decided since they were such nice fellows, we would be okay with them. Even though the driver who had transported us nearly begged us to return with him, we felt we were in good hands and left with them to go to the party.

There was some wine there, but I didn't have any. Mostly, we all just sat around and talked as we had done at Lil's Grill. When it got later, we decided it was time to go and they said they'd drive us, but on the way back, one of the sailors got a little too friendly with one of my friends. She told him to stop, and he did, but the driver of the car said we had to get out. We complied to make the point, but certainly didn't think they would leave us on the side of the highway in another city. It was after midnight.

Away they drove, leaving us behind. We thought they were just trying to scare us, and we kept thinking that until we couldn't see the taillights of their car any more. So we just started walking the 17 miles home, kind of afraid, but still thinking the boys would come back or a car would come along shortly.

But they didn't. In fact, no one did. So there we were, three little girls in our jeans and tennis shoes. We had wanted a grown up adventure, and what we got was a long, long walk out in the middle of a pitch black nowhere.

Hours passed. Our feet hurt, we were all crying, and we weren't even certain we were headed in the right direction. Then, about the time we thought we could go no further, we saw head-lights and all ran into the road to wave the driver down. As fate would have it, the driver of the on-coming car was a fellow we knew who was a waiter at a café in Virginia Beach.

"Margaret Bynum, is that you?" he asked, pulling up along-side us.

Greatly relieved, I acknowledged it was, indeed, me, and as we climbed into his car and drove away, I started telling him what had happened.

"Do you know how dangerous what you did was?" he asked.

We did know. And we also knew we'd never do anything like that again.

A few days later, one of the girls saw the sailors at a fast food restaurant near the YWCA. She came and told us, so we went to confront them about their ungentlemanly behavior, hoping to embarrass them in front of the crowd there. They took it like gentlemen, and were, in fact, very apologetic. So when they invited us to the formal military ball that was to be held in a few days, we agreed to go with them.

But, of course, we had other plans.

The sailors had said they'd be in their dress blues and for us to wear our best ball gowns. When they arrived, we'd gotten dressed, but in blue jeans and t-shirts and sneakers, just as we'd been when they met us and left us all alone in the middle of the road. They were so angry!

We said we'd just consider it even.

I had never been a confrontational person, but once in college, I did hit a personal wall and stood up for myself in a way I never had before.

At the time, I had been dating a Marine from Camp Lejeune who, I knew, was also seeing another girl. That was all right with me because I didn't want an exclusive relationship. Still, I had begun to have some feelings for this young man.

Because I was in school, he had to bring me back to the YMCA by 11 p.m. on Saturdays. One night, after a lovely evening together, he dropped me off, but then a few minutes later, I saw him pick her up – a girl who lived just down the hall from me. Not a student, she didn't have a curfew, and I became livid thinking of the fact that she knew she had my boyfriend's attention at a time – and likely in a way – I did not.

Worse still, she clearly knew I was the "Before 11 p.m." girl, and would come to my room and say, "Oh, Margaret, can I help you with your homework?" and "Oh, Margaret, is there anything I can do for you?" as if she was my best friend.

Once I realized who she was, I made it known to her that I wanted nothing to do with her, but she continued her solicitous behavior.

One Saturday afternoon, I say him drop her off, then a few minutes later she came to my room and said, "Well, hello. Isn't it such a nice day?" knowing full well she'd been seen and how that must have affected me.

"You can get out of my face, and I strongly recommend you do it now," was my reply.

Smiling sweetly, she came over and started patting the top of my head.

"Aww, Margaret," she cooed.

And I snapped.

I grabbed her arms as I pulled myself upright, and we began to physically fight. We fought all the way down the hall to the room where she lived, making a ruckus that brought all the other girls out to see what was happening.

She was taller than me, but very thin; I had always been a little chunky and although I had never fought like that before, I knew I was stronger. I caught both of her puny legs with one hand and threw open her bedroom window with the other as if I was going to throw her out. The other girls were crying, "No! Margaret, No!"

Of course, I didn't throw her out, but I like to think I scared her enough to behave more civilly in the future. Sometimes, you just have to make your point known, and although I would never condone fighting, I must say that was probably the angriest I have ever been at anyone.

— ◆ —

It wasn't all fighting at the YWCA, of course. There were lots of very nice girls and I developed some friendships that lasted throughout my years there, and well beyond. We also had some very fun times that I will always remember.

These were the years when I had more freedom than at any other time in my life, and I looked to expand my personal boundaries to the extent possible.

Of course, living at the YWCA, the level of freedom was less than, say, living in an apartment with no curfews or supervision.

The YWCA... Margaret's residence during college.

This is probably why my mother settled me there, but still, we girls were always looking for ways to have fun.

For one thing, we thought it would be fun to have a few nips of alcohol one evening. We put our pennies together and scrounged up enough cash to send one of the girls' boyfriends to the store for a pint of Four Roses. We waited nervously for them to return with the verboten potion, and were anxiously looking out the window when we heard their car pull up in front of the Y. My friend stepped out, took about five steps, and tripped, dropping the bag onto the paved driveway. Booze and glass went everywhere, thus ending our initial foray into college alcoholics.

We fared better with baked goods.

There was a bakery right nearby the YWCA and, to our delight, it was staffed by attractive young men around our age. They would toss pebbles at our window until we'd go to see what was happening, then when we came down to chat with them, they'd give us fresh bread.

Now that I think of it, those were certainly some great days.

➤ ◄

After I left the Y, I completed my college term renting a room with a woman I had met there who had gotten her own place. I can't think of any stories of particular interest related to that domestic arrangement, which is probably testament to the fact that I had learned a few things in my six previous residences.

I know that I learned to understand the importance of respecting other people's rules. And I learned that when you live under someone else's roof, it is important to be obedient whether you like it or not, and to be bold enough to ask questions about what is expected of you. I also learned not to take things to heart and the value of holding your tongue when you feel like gossiping, or when someone is speaking ill of someone else and you want to defend them; a wise woman stores information carefully, uses it judiciously, and chooses her battles wisely.

The academic rigor required at Norfolk was more than I had anticipated, but I was used to lagging behind. Still, I felt the college professors were more interested in helping me than my high school teachers. One in particular, Miss Bailey, was very encouraging. She was impressed with my typing and shorthand skills and suggested that I become a teacher instead of a secretarial science candidate. I adopted her as my mentor and would seek answers from her more than anyone at the college.

But all my teachers weren't so supportive.

I had to take a class called Tests and Measurements which, at the time, I felt was the most ridiculous concept ever. Only one professor on campus – Dr. Capps - taught this course and it got around school that most students did not pass. Thinking we were clever, several of us decided to take the course in the summer on the thought that she would be on vacation and someone else would be teaching. Imagine our shock when she walked through the classroom door and yelled, "Surprise!"

I think I earned a C, so I guess that was better than most.

My one non-academic endeavor at college was participation in the Drill Team. There were more than twenty female students who participated in competition and I enjoyed learning the movements and the routines. I was actually pleased with how well I'd done, especially based on my previous lack of academic prowess. I remember we were invited to be on The Ed Sullivan Show, but I don't remember why that never occurred. We did, however, perform at different colleges which was always a thrill.

I stayed on the drill team for less than two years. I would have gladly stayed longer, but because I had to work, I could not attend college full time as was required for inclusion.

I suppose boys could also be considered non-academic endeavors, and although I didn't have what most could considered an active dating life, there were a few notable individuals worthy of mention here.

The first fellow I shall mention, however, was probably the best dancer I have ever known. His name was Eddie and I met him at the drive-in restaurant and, at least for me, it was love at first twirl. Although he led me to believe we might have potential as a couple, I soon found he had another girlfriend. In fact, every time I called his house, whichever of his family members that would answer would call me by her name!

Another fellow who briefly stole my heart was a Navy man. My mother had told me to stay away from servicemen as they had life experiences and expectations far outside what I could consider appropriate. This was true with this fellow, as well. A few weeks into dating him, I found he had forgotten to divorce his wife!

Most of the boys I knew, though, were just my friends. We'd go out in groups, and sometimes there would be flirting, but really no more than that. People would try and fix me up with their friends and sometimes I would acquiesce, but it rarely turned out well. Once, I was introduced to a Navy man who, initially, appeared charming and very handsome to me. However, when he took off his hat, he was completely bald! I dated him several times and he was a fine person, but I couldn't get over that bald head. I know that now many young men shave their heads for fashion, but back then, a bald head meant you were old, and, although it may sound shallow now, back then I was not interested in dating an old man.

And then, there was the time I participated in a sit-in demonstration.

It was 1957-1958 and Jim Crowe was alive in the state of Virginia. The civil rights movement was in full swing in Norfolk, where I was attending college and other places in the south.

The schools, movies, restaurants, colleges had all been segregated and everyone knew "separate but equal" didn't mean anything. We had been treated as second-class citizens in many ways for many years. We could not eat at any restaurant unless it was owned by someone of the same race. We could not drink from the same water fountains nor could we use the same restrooms as non-Blacks. We couldn't even sit with the rest of the crowd at the movie theater. We had to sit upstairs while the Whites were downstairs. The only place that was not segregated was the drive-in theaters.

The public schools were closed down and the department stores made it obvious that they did not want our business. We couldn't try on shoes, including summer sandals, unless our feet were covered. We could not try on hats at all. We had separate beaches and of course our own place on the back of the bus. While traveling to and from college from my small hometown, we had to wait in separate waiting rooms and use separate restroom facilities.

So, about ten of us decided that after school one day, we would go to the segregated lunch counter at the downtown Norfolk Woolworth's and sit at whatever stools were empty.

I was one of the first to find a seat, and shortly thereafter, a White man came by and asked me to move. We followed the speaking of Dr. Martin Luther King who espoused non-violent revolution, and had agreed that our sit-in would be completely non-violent. Should someone ask us to move, we would not respond verbally, but would simply get up and wait for the next empty seat which we would then occupy. But before I answered, the man pushed me. He honestly didn't push me hard, but I guess I was so tense, I lost my balance and fell off the stool.

Remembering our decision not to respond, I just got up and

continued to wait with the others who were not seated yet. I don't remember finding another empty seat before we left the store, and when it was time to go, we all left quietly.

We didn't think the sit-in was a success at the time. Now, looking back, I can see how our efforts contributed to the integration of Norfolk. Perhaps even more so, however, were the efforts of the many military men who were stationed in the city and wanted their children to receive the best education the local public schools had to offer. They and their family's contributions to the economy carried a lot of weight, and Norfolk integrated quickly as a result. Other cities in Virginia did not fare as well with several closing for more than a year.

I think what I learned from the experience was that without support from people who are part of the system, nothing happens. I took this lesson with me years later when I wanted to promote to a civil service position and chose to take classes at Old Dominion College University, which was primarily an Anglo school, because so many people from there successfully got civil service jobs.

➤ ◄

It wasn't that far from home to the college, but no one from my family came to visit me. Initially, I went home for vacation, but, you know, it's never the same once you've made the move from home. As a result, each summer from 1957 to 1963, I sought and found a job to stay busy and make some extra money otherwise, I would have to return to Franklin and live with my parents. One summer, I got a job in New York on Long Island where I worked for several families cleaning their houses and babysitting their children. I even lived with one of the families who owned a bookstore in Long Island.

As I've written, I was a part time shampoo girl for two years. My next job was as a car hop at the little drive-in restaurant not far from the YWCA where I was living. I had to pay my own rent because my mother was frustrated with me for not being able to maintain living quarters. This wasn't one of those places where the servers had to wear roller skates, fortunately, but there were still opportunities for calamity

My job title was car-hop even though I waited on customers who were seated inside. The tips weren't bad for the prices we charged. I can still remember that milkshakes were $.40, a cheeseburger with fries and a soda were $.35. I don't remember what my starting salary was, but when I got a raise, I was making $.70 an hour. With that and my tips, I was able to pay my rent and buy a few groceries.

My career at that point also included assisting friends on their jobs. Once, a friend asked me to work in her place at a small restaurant. It was just for one day, and she told me that all I would have to do was to wash dishes for the lunch meals. But after the meals were done and the dishes washed, the boss dragged a 100-lb. bag of potatoes into the kitchen and asked me to peel them. I walked off the job and don't remember if my friend was fired or not, but I'm pretty sure she was.

My favorite college job, though, was working as a file clerk in a real estate office. It was the kind of clerical work I'd been told I'd never be hired for, and it was a pleasing thing to be able to prove those naysayers wrong.

The name of the firm was Collette Real Estate and their stock in trade was commercial property rentals. The owner was Maurice Collette and he said he saw something in me and would, therefore, give me a chance. So every day, I answered phones, and wrote some letters (although most of those had to be re-written because of my grammar) and did the filing. I also did filing in Mr. Collette's home office which was in his attic. He was into stock brokerage and I would file his reports and papers.

Mr. Collette saw to it that I had enough time for my school work and he fronted the cost of my tuition, taking a certain amount from me each pay day until paid in full. He also helped me with other school expenses, like books.

Because I could only attend part time, it took me seven years to finish college. But in 1963, at age 22, I walked in the ceremony and received my Bachelor of Science Degree in Business Education.

My mother and father were there to attend my Baccalaureate

ceremony and to see me receive my degree. I remember them being very happy for me. More so, I remember simply being happy to have completed my studies and move on with my life. I knew that degree, and the life experiences gained during my studies had given me more opportunities than my parents had been afforded, and I was grateful for that.

College had provided me with the soft skills I needed to handle a job, and increased my social skills to an extent. I say it that way because anyone who begins college at age 16 and without proper study skills is unlikely to make great decisions without guidance from home, as well as school.

To this day, my biggest regret about my college years is not applying myself to the extent I could have. Considering my choices alongside some of the students I have had over the years, I see how I could have taken the advice I was given more to heart and built a more straightforward career that would have benefitted a greater number of students.

In contemplating my path, I am reminded of a student who was told she would never make it in law school; however, she passed the bar on her first try. Another was told he was not Harvard material; however, he graduated in three years, and with honors. Another student received his doctorate after his counselor laughed at him when he mentioned he wanted to attend University of California, Davis. I think of them and then I think of the circuitous route I took to get where I should have gone much quicker. But I also recognize that the path we choose ultimately takes us to where we need to be.

Therefore, while my intent was to obtain a job teaching immediately upon graduation, after taking the Practicum, doing some student teaching, and taking the National Teachers' Examination, I was still extremely unsure about my ability to be a successful teacher.

Add my test-taking anxiety to my experience seeking a teaching position with the school leader from the Opportunity Home who wouldn't hire me even though he could have, and you can imagine how I felt, questioning my worthiness.

It would be years before I would change my mind.

Chapter Three

Who Said Education is Reserved for the Classroom?

Turn the other cheek so you can suntan evenly.
~Margaret Hill

No, I didn't become a teacher right off, although many people who know me probably think I've been involved in education my entire life. Instead, my first job after college was as a teller in a bank. But this was okay. Most of the other tellers only had high school degrees, so I knew my college degree was a consideration in my hiring. That's where I was when John F. Kennedy was assassinated and also when the leader of the Dominican Republic was killed.

That job as bank teller was both interesting and frustrating.

You see, I was the first Black teller that bank had, in fact, it is my understanding that I was the first Black to work at a bank in the entire state of Virginia, and I just don't think people trusted me with their money. For my first few months, I always felt like a monkey in the cage as I stood there looking at the long lines at the other teller's windows, yet no one wanted to come to mine.

But one by one, they began to trust me and, as you may know, my line became the long one in the bank.

I was at work one morning when members of the FBI came in and met with the manager of the bank. Because the bank was located on a military base, I did not think much of their visit. In fact, one naval payday, I jokingly said to a seaman who always cashed the checks for the men in his division, "With all this money, you can certainly take a nice vacation. " A few hours later, one of the men from the division came into the bank and asked if the seaman had cashed the checks and I told him yes, quite a few hours ago. I learned not to joke about money because he did keep the money and tried to leave the area but was caught at a local motel before he could get out of town.

That incident involved the FBI, local police and military police.

However, this particular morning, things were a little different, especially when the manager asked the teller in the cage next to me to lock up and follow him. He never returned so we all were concerned about what was going on. When the bank closed, we were told there was an investigation and we could not leave. We waited (about five of us) in this one lounge area for over an hour when we began to discuss what had happened. We had been told that money was missing but during our discussion, I stated perhaps $10,000 was missing. I was the first one interviewed by the FBI and the first question was 'Why did I mention $10,000 might have been missing?' It was just a wild guess, but it was also the second time in that job that I should have kept my mouth shut and didn't. This was my first and only time taking a polygraph test.

Obviously, I passed.

My boss at the bank, a retired Rear Admiral named Sweeney, suggested I go to school to learn the technology banks were beginning to use. I thought it was a good idea, and signed up for the all day Saturday test. There were seven or eight of us from various banks in the area in the course, and I felt good about my ability to excel in the class.

One of the things said to us before the testing was that we would each be notified of the test results and positions would be offered to the three with the highest scores. We were all pleased with that, but, in fact, only three out of the eight or nine of us completed the test in the allotted time. One of those students was me.

We were told that our managers would be notified in two to three weeks and, in one day, Dr. Sweeney came to me and told me I didn't make it. I thought that was strange because I was one of the few who had finished my test and I had felt confident in my answers, and I told him so. He said he thought that was odd, as well, and that I should follow up with the trainers, which I did.

Three weeks later, I still hadn't received a call, so I called them to ask how I had ranked. No one would tell me, so I asked to see the test answers, and they said no. Frustrated, I went to Dr. Sweeney and told him what had happened.

"You know as well as I do why you didn't get it," he said.

I realized there was no future in banking for me, so I left and never looked back.

I took the Civil Service exam, qualifying as a GS-2 which allowed me to apply for the position of keypunch operator. I had never seen a keypunch machine before, nor did I know how to operate one, so my boss said I couldn't have the job at the pre-scribed level, but I knew, if given the opportunity, I could do it.

"Make me a GS-2 and if I can't do the job after one month," I told him, "you can demote me."

He agreed and, in fact, by three months, I promoted to GS-3.

I worked there for about a year, then took a position at the Naval Air Station, working at the Commission Officers Mess Hall and Quarters. It was my job to assign people to housing, but this may not have been the right job for a girl with limited multi-cultural experience. I quickly learned you cannot house Muslims with non-Muslims, and I also quickly learned that it is difficult, indeed, to be a marriage counsellor when the wives would call looking for their husbands who I knew were drinking at the cantina.

I shared the rank with another female employee and we worked well together, quickly becoming the best of friends. Since

I lived over 50 miles from the job, she graciously opened her home to me. We were two young, driven women working in a predominantly male industry and that commonality bonded us more than the differences in our ethnicities could have separated us. Those were good days, but in Virginia in the early to mid-1960s, but there were still some things held over from more discriminatory times that ensured we'd never truly have the opportunity to spend our times as social equals. Perhaps the biggest example of this occurred the day my co-worker invited me to go horseback riding with her.

I have written about my experiences with ill-tempered farm animals, so it should not be a surprise that I was not much of a horseback rider. However, she loved it and wanted to share the experience with me. However, we found ourselves going from stable after stable consistently being told all the horses were out or either reserved. My friend didn't seem to realize what was happening, but I did. I just kept hoping we'd find a stable where they'd simply rent me a horse and we could go enjoy the day.

We finally arrived at a place where there were dozens of horses lined up in stalls ready to be ridden. My friend went to talk to the stableman and I stayed by the gate. I saw them talking, and saw him look over her shoulder at me. Shortly, she returned saying he'd been clear he would not rent horses to the both of us. I laughed and told her I knew this would happen after our first stop.

As I remember, we eventually found a stable but it was quite a ways from where we'd parked. The first time I rode my horse, Ginger, she ran away and I was helped by one of the farm hands. I don't think it was a prejudiced horse because for the next few months, I always rode Ginger. But I will always remember the look on my co-worker's face when it dawned on her what was happening that one day.

My co-worker and I continued to be good friends until I received the promotion that made me her supervisor. I suppose since we had been the same rank, she felt she deserved the same promotion and even though it wasn't mine to give, I bore the brunt of her frustration. She became very defiant and belligerent towards me and would be very rude in the presence of others. Compounding the non-job-related headaches of the position was the fact that I was having problems of my own... but more about those in a bit. Suffice to say that my work was suffering and I felt incompetent, so I left.

That, I never regretted.

My next position was at the Armed Forces Staff College. It was my job to make sure that all the officers being assigned to the college had housing and moving accommodations. My department was supervised by a Lieutenant Junior Grade whose last name was Loeser. He was a great supervisor and I enjoyed working for him.

I must be honest and say I did do a brief bit of teaching early on in my career. I was a substitute teacher in Virginia for a total of three days.

My job as a substitute teacher was to fill in for Kindergarten, fourth grade and fifth grade teachers who were ill. I liked teaching well enough, but the control required to manage a classroom of challenging students was something I was not yet prepared for. One day, during the morning prayer, I heard an unusual noise in the back of the room and looked up to see two fifth graders playing cards. It was prayer time and the beginning of the school day and they were playing cards. How does a person deal with that? I ceased substituting that day.

The skills I learned in my early career were helpful to me when I began working for the school district. I already knew how to be patient with staff, students and parents so I felt I was never at a loss for words and did not have a problem apologizing.

As we're discussing my years as a young adult, I suppose we should return to the discussion of my love life.

I met an interesting sailor from Pennsylvania once. Although he was short and kind of dumpy, I thought he was so smart and interesting but my limited command of the English language caused him to continually correct my speech. It was probably as frustrating for him as it was for me, and one day, he just disappeared.

I met who I considered my first real boyfriend while I was working at the drive-in restaurant and the beauty salon. He was in the Navy and was from Maryland. He trusted me with his vehicle when he went out to sea but he never seemed to hang around and I seldom saw him on weekends. I discovered he forgot to tell me he was married.

Then I met a fellow named Louis who was a Navy Chief. He was handsome and had a good sense of humor when he was in my presence and was a great dancer, something I'm not. We travelled together quite a lot, even going to Washington, D.C., New York and other places of interest on many occasions. My friends saw him as someone who was lacking social skills but I thought we were a great couple. But about that same time, Louis also met another woman who was a school teacher.

I found out they were dating and, although it upset me, Louis and I had made no commitment to each other. So, we'd still go out some and I continued to hope he might tire of her and return to me on a fulltime basis.

Imagine my surprise, then, when I went to work one day and found my co-workers talking about how they had read in the newspaper that my boyfriend was engaged, and certainly not to me. One said, "See, I told you he was no good." I was too upset to read the announcement, but determined to read it when I got home. But when I did, I found those pages of the paper had been removed, seemingly by Louis, my ex-and-now-engaged-to-a-school-teacher-boyfriend.

I took a bit of a break from dating after that. In time, though, I did meet someone: Walter who became my first husband.

We met because both our mothers had died. I know that is an odd reason to meet – perhaps, it should even have been a sign, but I didn't see it at the time.

A young lady at work became my friend and knew I was not dating. I was 25 years old at the time, and probably the only one of my friends that age who was not married.

Mary said, "Margaret, I'd like for you to meet my husband's cousin."

"Who is he?" I asked.

"His name is Walter and you both have something in common because his mother just passed away also," she replied.

I asked Mary to arrange for me to meet him, and she agreed to do so. The following day, Mary said, "Margaret, he wants to meet you. Are you willing to go by his house? He lives with his brother."

"Oh no," I said. "I'll have to meet him someplace."

So, we met at the funeral home where her cousin worked which was not far from my job. I know that's an odd place to meet, but we both knew where it was, and at the time, I guess it made sense. We introduced ourselves, chatted briefly, then, as planned, we went to dinner.

At the restaurant, we talked about our mothers and how we both felt as if we had lost our best friend. He told me he visited the cemetery every week at least once. I shared that I did not visit the cemetery, and he thought that was strange. I later learned his visits were out of guilt. I wish I'd done this and that, he would say. I had done everything I felt I could possibly do for my mother. My only guilt was the time she gave me permission to visit my friends in Norfolk and my payment to her was to visit my sick uncle. I was just 19 at the time and now I realize I had acted as though I was nine.

Instead of visiting Uncle John first, I went directly to my friends' place and hung out with them until it was time to get the bus home. We were having such a good visit, and somehow time slipped away. It wasn't until I was at the bus station that I realized I hadn't gone to visit Uncle John. Of course, when I returned home, my mother wanted to know how our visit had gone, how he was feeling so I lied and told her he was doing a little better. She was so pleased that she did not visit him the next day as planned, instead determining to go the following week. That was Tuesday, and Uncle John died on Thursday.

In my heart, I still pay for that lie.

I was working as a civil servant. I thought I was too old to have children, but this seemed the right time to transition into a new phase of my life. Walter had been a Marine, but now worked for Ford. We bought a house together in Chesapeake and set about to furnish it a few months before we got married; maybe to ensure the other would be there, maybe because neither of us wanted to be alone.

After a year and a half of dating, we became engaged and set a date for our wedding. I honestly don't remember him asking me to marry him but at the age of 27, I felt I was running out of opportunities especially if I wanted children.

Walter was a life-long Catholic and I was a Baptist, but then again, I wasn't attending church anywhere, so it didn't seem a terrible imposition to join and, further, I felt it would help ensure the success of our marriage. It meant a lot to him and, I think, it is what he felt his mother would have wanted. I took classes and was ready to walk down the aisle February 24, 1968. We invited a few people, but I don't remember writing vows or planning a party like young ladies do these days.

The wedding was scheduled for 9 a.m. and when I woke up, it was snowing. I do not ever remember snow falling in February in Virginia, but that day, it did. And it just kept falling.

While on the way to the car, I asked my sister, Viola, who had made my wedding dress, "Shouldn't I have something on my head?"

She was surprised that I hadn't purchased a veil, but with her seamstress talent, she quickly made a headpiece from the leftover material while we were enroute to the church. That put us a little behind, but not a lot, and we continued on to the church. We had to cross the railroad tracks to get to the church and, as fate would have it, a train with many cars was passing. It went on and on, and the snow fell lightly more and more. Long story short, I was 40 minutes late getting to the church.

I was so upset when we arrived thinking no one would be there, but they were. All our guests were seated, waiting, and I felt a little better until I was told Walter had not yet arrived. I knew, though, that he was with his cousin who only lived about ten blocks from the church and feared he'd changed his mind.

Had a man chosen to break my heart yet again?

So there I was, nearly an old maid sitting in her home-made wedding dress in the drafty Catholic church already upset about my late arrival and now teary-eyed over the thought that I might be left at the altar by a man who had taken my love for granted.

I was relieved when, less than a half hour later, he'd arrived – also claiming weather – and the ceremony went forward. I don't remember much about it, perhaps I was still too shook up from the events of the day, but I know I said nothing except "I do."

Walter said it, too, and that started a new phase in my life which – like everything else in this journey – has led me to where I am right now. But I'm clearly getting ahead of myself.

———

As I said, I was working at the Naval Air Station and Walter worked for the Ford Company. We were husband and wife, but his first love was playing craps; if there were any funds left, he paid the bills. It was not unusual for him to come home on a Friday and not have any money. I knew he gambled before we were married, but somehow I had felt marriage would make him want to change.

I don't know why people ever think things like that.

I think about those days while I was a principal and would always take the dice from my students when I saw them playing.

I never told them about my marriage or my husband's addiction to gambling, but I did tell them they had to wait until they could afford to lose the amount they wanted to play with. It's just common sense.

But common sense isn't common in everyone, and Walter continued losing most of his pay every week meaning that I bore the burden for our expenses. I decided, then, to take some drastic measures and quit my job in hopes that would shake him up enough to assume the responsibility of maintaining a home. I suppose I don't have to tell you what happened. But I will.

I remember the one Friday night that the electricity was turned off and they were not able to turn it back on until the next day. We lived in a three bedroom home in a new development surrounded by corn fields and vacant land and our house was the only one built in that block with the closest neighbors quite a walk away. We only had one automobile, but Walter decided to take it to go roll dice with the guys, leaving me alone – and quite terrified - in the dark. He was gone for five hours.

I should have seen the signs that this marriage would never work when he chose gambling over me. Our car was repossessed, and it didn't change him. Our refrigerator and riding lawn mower were repossessed, and he didn't even apologize. The only reason they did not take the air conditioning unit is because they would have had to cut a hole in the wall to uninstall it. I knew the house would be next, so I began to prepare for my future.

And it wasn't just the gambling. I was also aware of his fondness for other women.

At one point, I was taking classes at Old Dominion University, where I would go after leaving work at the Armed Forces Staff College. One night I just did not feel like taking the bus the 20 miles home, so I called a friend to drive me instead. It's wrong, of course, but I knew this fellow was interested in me, and that he would do it if I asked; I just did not feel like taking the long ride home on the bus.

"Oh my, what was in that food? I'm ill," I lied.

I need to get to a restroom and in a hurry," I insisted. "I can't even discuss how I feel. Take me home. Can't you drive faster than that?"

As we approached my house, I began to think he might want to be sure I was all right.

"Stop right here and don't pull into the driveway. I have to run in and use the restroom. Goodnight," I said, running to the house and quickly letting myself in.

I was in the bed faking a sleep when my husband entered the house less than five minutes after I arrived. He shook me several times, attempting to wake me for a serious conversation.

"What do you want?" I asked, trying to sound groggy.

"How long have you been home?" he asked.

"I was at school. I got home a little over two hours ago, same as always. Why are you waking me?" I replied.

"How did you get home?" he asked.

"The bus, same as always. What is wrong with you?" I said.

"I called but you weren't here." He lied.

"You know I have to work in the morning so let me get back to sleep," I said, ending the conversation.

Life has a way of making the playing field even and the next day when I asked him why he was so concerned about how I got home and what time I had arrived, I knew he'd never confess that he saw me because that would have led to questions he was unprepared to answer.

But I had no questions. I was done.

About a year later, I called Viola, my sister, who was living in Franklin, to inform her that I was leaving and that I would need assistance since I was not working. She's always protected me in the past, I knew she would again.

She said, "Come home and I will help you." So, gratefully, I did.

I borrowed five dollars for gasoline from my friend James, packed the car, and left for Franklin that day. Someone – and I've never known who – took it upon themselves to inform my husband that I was leaving and he called inquiring what I was up to.

"I'm just cleaning the house," I said.

"No, you're not," he replied sternly.

I hung up and jumped into the car, headed for my sister's. I knew he could not get off work and get home before I got out of the house, but I also knew he'd be looking for me as soon as the whistle blew.

Unfortunately, while traveling to Franklin, we passed each other on the freeway, going in opposite directions. I saw him and tried to duck my head, but he saw me first, making a U-turn, and the chase was on.

I knew he wasn't familiar with Franklin, so I didn't have a problem dodging him, hiding my car at the bus station. He headed for my sister's home, assuming I would be there, so I drove to my Uncle's farmhouse and parked, determined to wait him out. But at one point, I got so anxious, I had to call Viola.

When she picked up the phone and realized it was me, her tone changed. I knew he was there and asked her so.

"Yes, indeed," she said, pretending to be talking with someone else. I told her I'd stay at Uncle Randall's for a few hours and to stall him as long as possible so we wouldn't pass each other on the road again.

He waited, my sister told me, but when I didn't arrive, he left early that evening, later calling from home to apologize and ask if we could work things out.

But I had had enough, so I lied and said I would return home the next morning so we could talk after he got home from work. I am certain it was a shock to him when he got home that next night and I was not there.

My eldest sister, Viola Bynum Elam, made it possible for me to get to California.

Where I was, was on the Greyhound bus to San Bernardino, California, courtesy of the ticket Viola had purchased for me. It was 1969 and less than two years since our wedding day, and it took three long days to get there, but I felt free and ready to start fresh. I had no job, but my brother and his family took me in, and helped me find a job with Operation Second Chance.

It was a good life, quiet and work-focused. I felt I was helping people and using my degree. I stayed with my brother and his family for a while, but the San Bernardino heat was too much for me, so I travelled to San Francisco to visit my brother, Linwood, his wife and four children for a while until he got his orders to go to Alaska. To be fair to Linwood, he did ask if I wanted to go with him and his family, but I didn't think I'd like the Alaskan winters any more than the San Bernardino summers, so I returned to southern California.

Then one morning at 6 a.m., I got a call from Walter.

"I'm in Barstow and I'll see you soon," he said.

My eldest brother, Linwood Bynum, offered me a place with his family in Alaska.

I didn't know where Barstow was, so when my sister-in-law woke up, I told her he was headed here. She told me he was likely to arrive at any moment, and I didn't know what to do, but he hadn't sounded angry, so I wasn't afraid. I dressed, thinking of how I'd enjoyed my life in San Bernardino, but realized I was a little lonely. I thought maybe he'd made the long, long trip to California because he had learned his lesson and truly wanted to make our marriage work. So I fixed my hair and took a seat in the living room until he arrived.

➤ ◄

So, in 1970, we secured our own apartment in Del Rosa and Walter got a job in construction; at least that is what he told me.

I know he worked one day, but cannot say how many more. He would leave home and return after I went to work. When I found him at home a few times earlier than expected, it was always, "They let us off early today because we finished the job earlier." I guess he never thought the paycheck would indicate he had not been productive. I still wonder how stupid that man thought I was.

Admittedly, construction was not a good choice for him, Walter sought training as a cosmetologist. Unfortunately, he never pursued cosmetology work.

Still, I hung on. And he continued to tell me he was a changed man, he simply needed a little more time to find a career in California.

About a year later, he got a real job, working with the California Youth Authority. He said he wanted us to move out of the apartment and buy a house and a second car, so whatever tiny shreds of hope I'd held on to were reinvigorated, at least for a while.

We purchased a four-bedroom home in Rialto, bought a Ford Torino and a Toyota Corolla station wagon. It was 1971, and I had been working at Operation Second Chance for Frances Grice for about a year. I loved the job and what we were doing for young people, but one day, I was approached by a colleague on the School Board who asked why I was not teaching. I told him I had given it a try, but hadn't liked it. He reminded me that the school desegregation verdict in San Bernardino was in place.

"We need teachers," my friend said. "You can do this."

By then, I had abandoned my plans to ever teach again, and although I had submitted an application when I first came to California, I hadn't followed up with any level of persistence. So I filled out an application and within a week, I was hired at San Bernardino High School to teach recordkeeping and bookkeeping, later adding shorthand, typing, math applications, and English courses. The work was challenging and although people in the community who considered San Bernardino little more than a "prison school," I soon learned it was a place I felt needed and began to see the fruits of my labors in the faces of my students.

——▶ ◀——

We finally were bringing in enough funds to pay our bills, have friends over to play Pinochle, and go bowling at least once a week. We even had enough money to travel to Las Vegas once a month. My husband indulged in alcohol but not to the extent that he was violent. We socialized often by having family and friends over for holidays and weekends. Life was pretty good. Then I began to notice things.

I remember one night he said he was going to play poker with the guys and he did not return until the next morning. The give-away sign that he did not play poker all night long was when he came in at 7 a.m. and proceeded to cut the grass in the front and back yards. This was not the typical behavior of someone without any sleep.

Another time, he told me his job was requiring him to attend a workshop in Santa Barbara for the entire weekend. When he left at 5 p.m. on Friday, of course, being the good wife that I was, I walked him to the car to say good-bye, but I also took a reading of the speedometer. The give-away sign was when he returned about 10 a.m. Sunday and had only traveled 14 miles.

One Christmas Eve, he came home about midnight with a large box for himself with a jacket in it. When I asked where the jacket came from, he told me he purchased it, but there was gift-wrapping tissue paper – not store tissue paper – around the garment in the box.

In fact, my first husband always got caught in anything he did wrong. Once, he stayed out all night on a Saturday and the next morning, I had had enough and decided we discuss his behavior. Resigned to the fact that he was not going to change, I told him we were adults and should act accordingly.

"Where were you last night?" I asked.

"I was playing poker with friends," he replied.

"I'm sure you were out with a female. Why don't you admit it?" I insisted.

"Until you see me with someone, don't accuse me," he stalled.

"That is reasonable," I said. And I knew it wouldn't be long before I did.

In fact, it was that same day.

CHAPTER FOUR
Teaching for Good

You don't need the sharpest knife in the drawer to spread kindness.
~Margaret Hill

But enough of that. How you know me, likely, is through my work in education, so let's talk about that for a while.

I began teaching fulltime at age 31 and have taught a variety of courses at a number of schools and colleges. As discussed, I gave substitute teaching a try, but didn't like that. The impermanence of simply walking into someone else's class for a limited time was not how I saw myself best able to assist others; but that didn't mean I ever truly dismissed the idea of teaching.

On my way to building a legacy in education, I tried out a number of options. For instance, one summer after my first year of teaching, I worked in Santa Ana for Reverend Leon Sullivan's program which was called OIC. My job was to assist students so they could pass the General Education Diploma (GED) test. This was an adult program so the ages of the students ranged from 18 to 70.

Up to that point in my education career, I hadn't even seen a GED book and was not fully informed as to what would need to be covered or the level of effort the students would be required to exert. Instead, I did the next best thing: I went to the courthouse in Orange County and took the test. Reading through the questions, I saw much of it was either basic scholastic content or common sense, so after passing the first three of five tests given, I felt I had enough knowledge to make a difference.

Some of my students had been out of the classroom for many years, but now knowing what they would need to learn, I soon found that you could, indeed, teach older students new tricks. We covered what was needed to pass, and as much of the supporting application and theory as I could fit into a class and when all was said and done, 14 of the 17 students entrusted to my care received their GED certificates. That meant 14 more people in the world who could now apply for jobs, or consider junior college, or career training. That meant 14 more people who could point to an achievement – however delayed – about which they could be proud. That meant 14 more people with hope.

I have held three full time jobs in San Bernardino for the 40 years that I have worked in San Bernardino. As I mentioned, I was first at Operation Second Chance, and then the San Bernardino City Unified School District. My last full time position was with San Bernardino County Superintendent of Schools Office. This was my first opportunity to work fulltime with young people and it was here that I was able to actualize what I then knew to be my calling as an educator.

At Operation Second Chance, a community-based job-training center formed in 1967 to provide training and jobs for youth and young adults on the west side of San Bernardino was founded by civil rights activist Frances Grice. Our students lived on the Westside of San Bernardino and most of their dreams were nightmares. Our collective attempt was to provide hope for a future for them. Operation Second Chance was many things to many people but it was mostly about giving people in a low socio-economic area an opportunity to have a better quality of life.

And also, as I've mentioned, during my second year at Operation Second Chance, I had the opportunity to meet a school board member who learned I had a teaching credential which led to my first teaching position at San Bernardino High School. I was hired to teach recordkeeping, bookkeeping, shorthand and typewriting. I later taught math, English, career exploration and retail merchandising.

After I got hired, I was teased by people in the community who said, "Oh, you will be working in the prison school." I was frightened by those comments – what had I gotten myself into? - but soon I learned that was the place I wanted to be and the students became my friends as evidenced by the fact that many of them continue to stay in contact and visit me from time to time. As a matter of fact, I feel like the grandmother to many of my former charges.

In *It's All About the Children*, I wrote about many of my experiences working directly with

Cover of my first book, *It's All About the Children*.

students. Here, I'd like to talk more from the perspective of an educator and school administrator and how my own life was shaped through interaction with others through those years.

First, you should know that there were many people who supported me, but not all.

I can remember a fellow educator who removed departmental
resources from my classroom in another department. I'm not sure
if he didn't want me to succeed or was just severely lacking in
sharing skills, but when I needed paper, or pencils, or worksheets,
or anything else, it was regularly missing. My response was to
create my own worksheets and teach from those. Can't say it
made him happy, but my students were able to learn just fine.

I can also remember applying for tenure and finding the vice
principal had been busy doing all he could not to let that happen.
Thinking back, I believe it was because of my lack of grammar
skills – and perhaps he had a point – but when I was invited back
the next year to teach shorthand, and other subjects, I was elated
at being tenured and he and I never discussed why or why not
that may have been. So, perhaps, not so good of a point.

Of course, there were many good people, too. I remember
that in 1975, when I was part of a protest over teacher salaries, I
came into contact with one of those. We called it Teacher Dignity
Day where several teachers and some students marched with our
signs in front of the school district office. My vice principal told
me I'd likely have my pay docked for participating, but I felt the
cause was just, so I continued marching. He said if I ran short
of money, to see him and he'll help me out. I didn't need any
financial assistance, but I do remember how appreciated I felt
from the gesture.

In 1978, I went to the district office as a hearing panel member,
which is where I stayed until I got my masters and administrative
credential in December of 1980 from Cal State. But before I talk
about what happened after that, I want to share a little story about
my credential and how I learned to always check expiration dates.

When I was taking classes to complete my California credential, a school district classified employee named Jill was
always there to help with questions and informed me what
I needed to do from year to year in getting a clear credential
since my teaching credential was administered in the state of

Virginia. That staff member retired and I assumed her replacement would do the same. I completed all coursework and had submitted my paperwork and was glad that process was over. One day, the replacement staff member called me and said I needed to call the school district right away... my credential had expired. While I saw this as important, I was so naïve at the time, I didn't realize what it meant until she told me I couldn't resume teaching until I had a clear credential and the school would request a substitute for me until this issue was resolved.

I was working at San Bernardino High School at the time, and called the principal right away, explaining I had completed all coursework but the County/State did not have record that I had cleared my credential. It was about 4:30 in the afternoon, so I took a chance and called the State Department of Education and the director of credentialing answered the telephone. When I shared my dilemma, he cleared me to teach but I had to resubmit the necessary paperwork the next day, along with a processing check. Perhaps he sensed the utter terror in my voice, but he was so understanding; he called the school and said I met all requirements and that they were going to renew me. But can you imagine? Not looking at the expiration date on my credential filing might have meant I couldn't have been a teacher at all.

I taught at San Bernardino High School for seven years, and I am proud of each one. I allowed my students to establish rules and they followed those rules. In one class, the students were very bright, but also very challenging, and they were determined not to abide by the rules for homework. I told them one day that they must all turn in their assignments the next day and if they didn't arrive with their homework in hand, they were not welcomed in my classroom. I had referrals prepared, so if they turned in the assignment they took a seat, and if they didn't turn in an assignment, they received their referral and was sent to the office.

In seven years, with the exception of this assignment, I issued fewer than ten referrals and not a single suspension.

Mostly, I believe this was because I called the parents.

It is not the job of teachers to raise people's children. I have always believed this, and I probably always will, but we all know how little some teens communicate about much of anything, especially if they are having issues at school. So once when I had a particularly disruptive young man in my class, I called his father who ran a gas station in town. Less than ten minutes later, the man was standing in the doorway to my classroom asking if he could come in. I said yes, watching the look on his son's face change from one of smugly in control to surprise and concern. When the father arrived, I escorted the student outside my classroom where the father approached him and pushed him against the wall in the hallway all the while firmly explaining that his disruptive behavior was no longer going to be tolerated.

I never had to call that boy's father again. As a matter of fact, I don't believe I had to call a single parent in that class about their student's disruptive behavior.

———

I have always tried to keep my students interested in technical skills and prepared for the entry-level jobs I hoped most would seek right out of high school whether or not they went on to higher education. I believe young people need to learn the value of work from an early age, and to develop the skills they will need to work well with others as adults. I have also always tried to approach teaching from a practical perspective.

I have written several courses. One was called Career Exploration and in that class we looked at a number of different job opportunities. We would visit places to see various jobs in action. Once we went to the farmer's market in Los Angeles. My students also discussed going into business for themselves. We would hold mock employment interviews where the students would critique each other. I still remember one student who set a memorable example for the class.

This student had a full head of cornrows. He was bright and personable, but I knew that hairstyle was going to be an impediment to his job seeking. One day, he came to class and announced he had a job interview.

"Don't even go unless you're prepared to cut that hair," I warned.

But he said it wouldn't matter. So I asked the class what they thought of his chances. Their answers – like his results – were negative.

Life gives you these little teachable moments, I guess. Several years later, when I was the principal at San Andreas High School, I can still remember a student who came to me with a sad look one morning.

"What's wrong?" I asked.

"I got stopped by the police last night. I wasn't doing anything wrong." he said. "I didn't think the police could stop and harassed you if you are not speeding and not breaking the law. I am usually just a few blocks from my home and have not been speeding. I have a driver's license and my car is registered. Do you think they stopped me because my car is old and maybe I had the music a little too loud?"

I responded, "Don't you think it is time to get a haircut so that the police will leave you alone? A lot of people are driving old cars and the music is too loud in most of the cars driven by anyone under the age of twenty-five."

"There's nothing wrong with my hair. I have a right to wear dreadlocks."

"The police have a right to stop you also," I said, adding, "If you don't want to get a haircut, stop driving and have someone provide your transportation."

I received a stare that inferred, 'That's a dumb comment,' but two weeks later, the student had a nice clean haircut and we both chuckled.

"Tired of the police, I see."

"Yes, Mrs. Hill. I'm going to see if you know what you are talking about."

This student never received a ticket nor was he stopped by police for the remainder of his school career.

I attempted to let all students know that life might not be fair but no one ever said it would be.

$$\longrightarrow \longleftarrow$$

Once, I was asked to teach a math class. I hadn't studied the topic and certainly hadn't enjoyed it in school, so this was less than a stimulating prospect for me. Still, I knew the class needed to be taught, so I began considering the ways in which I could make it something from which the students could find both immediate and long term benefit. I constructed math problems based upon analogies related to cooking, and football, and other things they knew about already, and the response was very positive.

I was very pleased and the students all arrived on time, ready to learn. Maybe this is what upset the teacher with whom I worked in the adjacent classroom so much. Yes, this is the one I mentioned previously who removed my resources!

He was also a math teacher, and maybe he didn't consider my math background on the same level as his, but that really wasn't his call to make. Still, one day, every paper was missing from the cabinet. I was prepared to teach as usual, but without resources, an immediate response was needed in order that these fragile students retained their growing level of interest. Thinking fast, I told them all to take out a blank sheet of paper and to write what they wanted to learn. I gave them plenty of time to think about it, and when they were done, we went around the room and talked about what skills related to the things they'd listed. I ended up being able to focus my future lessons better and my students felt valued because a teacher had asked their opinion.

$$\longrightarrow \longleftarrow$$

Another time, I was assigned to an English class. Imagine – the subject that almost kept me from tenure, and I was asked to teach it! I was nervous that first class, but determined to be honest with the students.

"You need to learn English and so do I, so we're going to learn it together," I told them. I'm not sure they believed me, but I am sure we all benefitted from that class.

One of my English students, a young man named Sheldon, was a particularly talkative fellow. Unfortunately, his chattiness was usually while I was trying to teach, so since he was clearly familiar with everyone in the class, I gave him the job of class recorder. He would keep track of those who had been absent and help catch them up while I was working with the rest of the group. Problem solved, and Sheldon showed himself as a natural leader. I understand he retired from the Sheriff's Department. I hope the course helped him write his police reports.

The class was on a Thursday and I began to note a paucity of completed assignments. Students showed up with partial work, yet they seemed to understand the subject, so one day, I asked why.

"Are you all staying up late watching Johnny Carson?" I asked.

"No ma'am," said one. "We all watch Night Gallery."

While that explained the problem, it didn't solve it, and I knew I was unlikely to change their television viewing, so I asked them to write about what they watched, providing a different ending. They were so excited to share what they had written that I took it a step further and showed them silent 16-millimeter films. They were to write about what they were watching, thus building their abilities to translate visual to critical thinking skills. Again, they loved the work and I watched the quality of their writing improve exponentially. Today, we have all these standards, but my students probably used more than in other classes because they were really involved in what was going on.

These are some of the students with whom I still keep in contact. Derek, who is now Events Manager at the National Orange Show was in my retail sales class. One of the fellows who put on a school-wide fashion show for that same class now lives in Las Vegas where he owns his own business. Another young lady is an airline cabin attendant who recently told me she remembered feeling like a "real student" when she was in my class.

———

Two years later, in July of 1980, I became Vice Principal at Curtis Middle School where I stayed until 1983.

One thing about middle school students is that one day they can be angels, and the next, they can get on your last nerve. I remember one such young lady, but recently I ran into her at an event and introduced her to some of my colleagues.

"The only reason I got to be successful is because of this lady," she said, indicating me. "I was with the wrong kids and a bully telling everyone what to do and she said, 'If you want to be a leader, then come on, you can be in charge of the ASB.' She focused my skills in a positive direction."

———

Anyway, I learned a lot about people at Curtis. I had been around a lot of different types, but one young man's father – a member of the Hell's Angels – was a first for me. His son had been a continual problem: disruptive, failing to bring in homework, non-participative in class, and mean to other students, so I told him I was going to call his father.

"No, you're not," the boy said. "My dad's with the Hell's Angels."

But, of course, I had to if I wanted to help the student. Still, I was worried for my safety. But when the father arrived, dressed in his leathers with scarred knuckles and visible tattoos, he greeted me politely and listened attentively as I explained the situation. When I was done, he agreed the boy's behavior was inappropriate and promised he would speak with him about better following the rules. Clearly, I had misjudged him because of his bike club affiliation. But I learned that day that not all Hell's Angels are hell raisers and I promised myself I'd try harder at not being judgmental without reason.

➤ ◄

There was a time – and I have thought a bit before deciding to share this with you – that I did something as a teacher about which I am not proud. What I decided was that because I learned from it, others may also, and be able to use my example as one from which they can also learn.

Once, a young man was sent to my office for being disruptive in class. I saw how this was an issue immediately as the volume of his voice got louder and louder as we spoke. I tried to calm him speaking in a low voice and maintaining eye contact, but had no luck, so I took him outside where his protests wouldn't be disruptive to the people in the adjoining offices.

"You're disrupting class and, more so, your own education," I said.

I knew he rode the bus to school, so I told him he was not to return to class, but, instead, to wait right where he was, then be the first one on the bus.

He stood there, quiet at last, until I turned to go back inside.

"Shut up, nigger," he said, and something snapped in me. I turned and grabbed him by his collar, catching him by surprise. I was about to dump him over the railing when my Principal showed up, quickly disengaging the child. About a week later, I heard there was a fight and ran to help. The participants were two male students, one Black and one White.

As I arrived, the Black boy punched the White boy in the face exclaiming, "He called me a nigger." I told him that just because someone calls you a name, it is not a reason to be physical. I sent him to my office telling him to wait on one of the chairs outside my door while I attended to the other child. However, then I realized I'd sent him to sit next to the kid who had called me the same thing the previous week. I had to run back and move him!

I tell you this story because it is obviously wrong to be physically demonstrative with a student, regardless of your own feelings. I knew this at the time as well as I know it now. I wanted you to know that it is okay to feel angry – we all feel angry – but you cannot change behaviors or beliefs by acting on anger. As it turns out, that young man and I eventually became friends. I didn't give in, and he began, I suppose, to see me as a strong person, not just a Black person.

I was fortunate to have an understanding Principal, and when I became an administrator, I did my best to be understanding to my teachers, as well. I also did my best to be creative in the ways in which I dealt with students because, like my Principal, I realized positive things can happen when people are both made aware of the rules and allowed appropriate latitude.

There was once a group of students who would ride the bus to the school site, but then scatter in every other direction upon arrival. At the end of the day, they would return to the bus, and get their free ride home. Obviously, this benefitted no one, so I needed to find a way to make it stop quickly. What I did was to position myself at the bus door and those students who had not been in class or had not come directly from the school were not allowed on the bus.

It was a long walk home for many of the students, but, amazingly, attendance significantly improved.

I did a lot of things as an administrator that would likely get me reprimanded today. But the students learned the rules, recognized what would be tolerated, and did not push the boundaries they came to learn.

After Curtis, I went to Serrano Middle School for two years and there were teachers who wouldn't even talk to me. One man would pass me in the hall and, although I would say hello to him, he wouldn't acknowledge me. So on Mondays, Wednesdays, and Fridays, I'd greet him, and on Tuesdays and Thursdays, I would not. It took him about a year before he questioned me about this, beginning our ability to converse.

It was at Serrano that I interviewed for my first principalship.

I thought I had a good chance to secure the job, but it went to another candidate. They told me they thought I simply wasn't ready, and they probably were right.

But I've always been one of those people who will not try something more than once. If I don't get it, it's not to be and I accept that. People said not to give up, but I didn't feel that was what I was doing.

As fate would have it, a few years later while I was working as a vice principal at Serrano Middle School, the Deputy Superintendent spoke to me about serving as vice principal at San Bernardino High School, stating recently they'd interviewed people for the position and none were selected. He asked if I was interested, and I was, but I was also true to my standard of not trying twice when once did not work.

"I won't apply," I told him, "But you can assign me."

So he did.

After Serrano, I transferred back to San Bernardino High School. I started on July 1 and two weeks later, found I needed to have a hysterectomy and would be out for four weeks. I remember being in my office and having an upset stomach. I was in so much pain, I made an appointment to see my physician who patiently listened as I talked about the beef sandwich I had eaten at the deli across the street and how I had been warned that old meat usually becomes barbecue and how I regretted having eaten that. My doctor listened patiently and then told me it wasn't the sandwich and I had to have surgery and he would arrange it for the following week. What a surprise!

When I returned, people were wonderful, welcoming and

accommodating and the next two years held many experiences, both good and bad.

Once, a teacher came to my office in tears, reporting her purse had been stolen.

"I had cash in my wallet," she sobbed.

I told her to go back to class and I'd look into it, which I did, beginning with searching the grounds for the purse. It was quickly located on stairs leading to the fire escape exit, but there was no money in the wallet. So I went to the classrooms of every student in that building who had received a hall pass so far that period. Each was back in class with one exception. So a school guard and I went to the closest target of opportunity – the McDonald's down the street. There the young man was, with a group of friends and a table full of food.

"Where did you get the money for all this?" I asked?

"My dad gave it to me for doing work," he said.

I asked him to produce the McDonald's receipt and empty his pockets. Not surprisingly, the amount added up to the sum that the teacher said had been in her wallet.

The guard took the other students back to campus while I drove to the young man's home. His father was outside painting the porch when I arrived. I explained the situation and inquired as to whether he'd actually earned the cash.

"That boy hasn't helped me do a darned thing," his father said. "I certainly didn't give him any money."

Obviously, he had to pay the money back and apologize to the teacher, and I am certain his father disciplined him at home. One would think that would have put a stop to such behavior, but it wasn't long after that – at age 18 when he was attending San Andreas High School – he called me collect from jail. There wasn't much I could do for him, although I did offer to give him the homework assignments.

"Do you think they're going to give me a pencil here?" he asked incredulously.

Actually, I've had a lot of calls from students in jail over the years. I've always done all I can to help because I believe every kid deserves a chance in life, if only to know there is someone they can call. Dr. Herb Fisher used to say, "As fast as we kick a kid out of the back door, Margaret is letting them in the front." But I wanted to keep my students in school, and reform those for whom that was possible.

Once, at San Andreas, I was told about a student who was selling drugs out of the back of his truck in the school parking lot. The fellow implicated was a good-looking, clean-cut kid and I hardly would have suspected him, but there he was, repeating the same action each day. Students would come up to him, there's be a quick handshake exchange, and they'd be gone and he'd head back to class.

I decided to put him out of business, so I would go to his classroom at the end of each period and shadow him during his 15 minute breaks, then I would shadow him to his next classroom. I did this for a couple of weeks until one day, he just didn't come back.

As far as I knew, he didn't finish school, but one evening I was watching the television news and there was his picture as a recipient of the Medal of Honor for restraining a suspect for the police.

I could hardly believe my eyes.

➤ ◀

Students sometimes simply make bad choices. Sometimes, it's accidental. More often, it is because they are still of the mindset that they are immortal. One day at San Andreas, nine students found this was not the case.

The driver, a male student with no license, was likely trying to show off, or maybe he just wanted to scare the eight girls in the bed of the truck he was driving which belonged to the custodian, but he sped off campus to the store way too quickly, braked too hard, and rolled the vehicle catapulting all of them across the roadway. Bodies were everywhere and along with the fast-responding police cars and ambulances were news vans. As Principal, it was my job to put on my calm and professional face and speak for the school, but I was unable to stop crying. The girls were all badly injured and I was so afraid some of them would die.

None did, but the trauma marked the school for years after, and my own heart forever.

━━▶ ◀━━

Whether as a teacher or administrator, I have always been one to know who my students are and to be visible. It is important to see the dynamics of what is going on at a campus.

One day, I saw a vehicle parked by the cafeteria. One of our students, a young man named Albert, was looking nervous, and staring at the driver who appeared to be about 20 years old. I approached the car and told the driver I would allow him to be on campus but he needed to park elsewhere. I didn't say anything to Albert, and he quickly walked back to the building and the young man returned to his car and drove away. Later, a girl told me I couldn't have stepped in at a better time. The boy in the car was going to shoot Albert.

Why, I have never known, but fate has repeatedly put me in the path of more than one troubled student. Many of my high school charges lived in what I consider 'Survival Mode' where their day-to-day concerns were centered more on just making it through than their studies.

Because of the gang activity in my district, students were not allowed to wear baseball caps on campus. Especially concerning were caps constructed in gang colors. Still, many brought them to school.

I told them not to have the caps visible in the classroom, but one day, a student commented about the clothing of another.

"Those are gang colors," he said.

I responded, "I don't care what you're wearing as long as it conforms to school rules, but once you lay a hand on someone, you have to deal with me." The obvious things don't matter. You can take them all away, and the kids will still find ways to differentiate themselves, as this next example illustrates.

On one occasion, there was a good deal of gang 'color-wearing,' and it was causing concern among both students and teachers. I called the participating students' parents and said their sons' clothing was causing an issue, and for the next week, they had to wear a button down shirt and a necktie. To make sure they were in appropriate attire, I took neckties to school for them. The parents complied, but the other students liked the look so much, they wanted me to adopt the attire fulltime, and everyone still knew why they were wearing it.

I hired a counselor who had been a former gang member. She taught me a lot about what to look for in terms of gang activity. I remember once she came to me and said there was going to be a fight. I had always felt I had a strong grasp on the environment, so this threw me momentarily.

"How do you know?" I asked her.

"I saw a girl changing her hair style in a car," she said, explaining that was a clear sign of impending fisticuffs.

Sure enough, the student was called to the office and told us about the planned fight. You just have to know what to look for.

➤ ◄

Another strong belief of mine is that you must be authentic with students. They need to know why you are asking them to learn or do something. I do not believe anyone ever became successful solely because of a textbook; students become successful because of people who care about them.

As a teacher, I seldom used the textbook because I felt students would be more inclined to participate in the coursework if I used practical applications. I taught applicability and experience, with the textbook as a reference for those things. I believe it is the responsibility of the student to read the textbook at home and come to class prepared to discuss what they learned. School should be for research and refining what they need to know. My big problem as a teacher is that some of us don't teach... we read from textbooks.

At San Andreas, I had a sign on my door that said WE TEACH STUDENTS, NOT CURRICULUM. Not everyone liked that, but I didn't take it down because it is what I believe. There is a shared responsibility between the family and the school, and it has to be honored on both sides. Parents have to be firm. Sometimes, they have to ask the tough questions to know what is going on in their child's life. At Curtis Middle School, a parent once blamed me for his daughter's drug overdose.

"I know you are concerned about who gave the drugs to your daughter," I said. I'm also concerned about how she is doing. I'm going to pray for her and I know you will also." Sometimes, that's all you can do.

Parents have to put their children first. I have always thought that if you are blessed with children, you have the obligation to be there for them, but so many times, I have seen this is not the case. At Serrano Middle School, there was a young girl who always arrived late for her first period class and, for that reason, one day she was sent to my office. When I asked her about her habitual tardiness, she told me she had to get her younger siblings dressed and to school because their mother was always so loaded on cocaine she couldn't do it. Of course, I told her I would have to call Child Protective Services; but the girl said that if I did that, she would take the children and run and none of them would be able to attend school. I knew she wasn't lying, but for months, I was worried about being out of compliance and could lose my credential for not reporting her. I called the home often and felt comfortable that the student might have exaggerated a little.

A similar incident happened at San Bernardino High School. A 13-year-old freshman had gone to a friend's birthday party on a Sunday afternoon and didn't return until early Thursday morning, around 4 a.m. When she did return but said she was too tired to go to school, her father punished her by hitting her with a belt. Her sister told a school counselor at an elementary school and before I had a chance to do so, that principal called Child Protective Services. I spoke to the girl and she admitted that the story was true, but she said it was a single hit which is why she had said nothing. I gave her a piece of paper and told her to write down, in detail, what had happened, then I went to the Principal with the paper. A few hours later when I honored my invitation to attend a Christmas program at Serrano, someone called Child Protective Services saying I'd violated child abuse laws. Child Protective Services representatives and a city police office met with the student, as well.

"Tell Margaret never mind," she said the officers had told her. "She did the right thing."

Parents have to have rules. They have to say you can play when you finish your homework, you can give up your lunchtime recess to study, but so many don't. Today, there are so many diversions available to kids, but who puts them there?

Once, I had to meet with a teacher who was frustrated because her kids constantly texted each other on their cell phones in class. She didn't know what to do, but felt she had tried everything. I said, okay then, make the cell phones work for you. Pair up the students and have them send answers to each other over the phones, then hold up the phones with the right answers. They could still text, but they would also learn.

I believe cell phones have an educational capacity we have not begun to tap into. Similarly, school websites should have resources for people to get additional learning. But we have to show how these things will benefit the users. Our young people are demanding that from us and it is up to us to grow our teaching styles to meet that very intelligent and reasonable demand.

➤ ◄

I once filled in for a teacher who needed coverage for her class until she arrived, but found there were no assignments for the students to complete. There were, however, newspapers available, so we read those. We found and discussed weather region-wide. We talked about distance and travel. The students were so engaged in their discussion, they didn't want to discontinue the assignment when the teacher arrived. They were learning great research skills from something as simple as a newspaper.

Truly, I enjoyed teaching so much. We were always exploring, but it was never, ever "just read the book."

———— ————

I didn't teach in the public schools for the entire 32 years. For two years, I was a member of the District's Hearing Panel. There, my job was to work as part of a team of three to evaluate the reason a particular school was recommending a student for expulsion as well as listen to the student's version of what happened. We tried, as much as possible, to be impartial and make the most appropriate decisions as to whether the student should remain at the same school site, transfer to another school site, or dismissed from the district for a period of time, up to one full school year.

Although my intent was to make a positive difference in the lives of these troubled youth, the two years I served in that capacity were the most dismal in my career. This is primarily because, as you may imagine, hearings are not held for positive reasons. Marijuana was gaining in popularity, and regardless of the offense, so many parents were adopting the perspective that their children could do no wrong. Accountability was a rarity. When the opportunity to promote to school administration became available, I quickly took my leave.

———— ————

I have mentioned teaching in the evenings at college. One was the University of Redlands. My first student evaluation garnered me

19 "Excellent's," two "Good's," and one "Unsatisfactory" because I didn't make the class reach each and every chapter. From then on, I'd introduce myself to a new class with the caveat that if they wanted to go chapter to chapter and write papers, they were in the wrong class. It wasn't that I didn't want them to write papers – they wrote papers – it was because I wanted them to do more: to think deeply, to consider, to engage. When grading papers, I'd make a list of the issues I saw in all the papers and share that. I wanted everyone to be able to learn from each other.

My students were all future principals and vice principals, so we'd do a lot of role playing. They'd take the role of someone of another race, or gender, or someone from a radical group and have to argue their side of an issue. Afterwards, they would tell me, "Now I understand why it was done that way." Teachers cannot teach unless they can understand. You have to spend time with people unlike you to be able to recognize the warning signs that point to future issues, be they scholastic or otherwise, then you have to have the skills to take action.

———◆ ◆———

As you have read, I have always made it a point to talk with parents when I felt they should be a part of student problem-solving. And I have given you examples of parents who took that responsibility seriously, but as we both know, many do not.

Parents make excuses.

As an aware educator, you can see things coming, so you're not shocked when they manifest themselves in a student's behavior. Parents should do the same. Patterns are being formed when children are young, and those patterns are difficult - if not impossible – to break. Teachers are bound by the law, but parents need to recognize there is a difference between punishing and beating, and they need to be responsible to parent, which often means to punish.

———◆ ◆———

We have miss-educated our kids on life, and we have to do better so they can do better.

A young man in the Conservation Corps once came to a school meeting to speak about some of his classes.

"I am one of those people who doesn't like to go to school, but I understand you have a lot of good programs and I hope I can take advantage of what's going on. I know there are a lot of young people who feel that way. We don't always do things A-B-C, but we do want to learn."

I believe that young man does speak for many others and that young people sincerely do want to learn. It is up to educators to hear what they are saying and respond in a way that respects their desire to be educated. Times have changed and even standardized teaching doesn't place the teacher under a tree with students at their feet. We need to take a lesson from history and

recognize the good that can come from embracing the exciting technology now available.

While working as a principal, I also worked at Cal State University San Bernardino teaching Public Relation for School Leaders. It was an enjoyable experience, especially as most of my students worked as coordinators, counselors, or the like, and wanted to become administrators. The class gave them an opportunity to walk in the shoes of the students they worked with on a daily basis. We dealt with public relations incidents that were happening on campuses on a daily basis and worked as a team to develop

Receiving an Honorary Doctorate from the University of Redlands.

strategies on the best way to solve them.

One day, Bob Denham who was the Dean of Education at the University of Redlands sent a university graduate student to shadow me. Afterwards, I told her about my work at Cal State and how rewarding I found it. The following day, Bob called me and asked, "Why are you working for Cal State when you need to work for me?"

He gave me a list of classes and I chose Personal Development which focused on hiring, discipline documentation and dismissal practices. This, also, was a hands-on class. We dealt with situations that were occurring on campuses as we met. Some students were reluctant to talk about those situations but we made a confidential pack that we would not discuss any scenarios outside of the classroom.

Dr. Fischer, former San Bernardino County Superintendent of Schools, asked me to come to San Bernardino County Schools not long after. I was hired as a consultant on a part-time basis for about three months, then I was offered the position of Interim Assistant Superintendent which I held for about two years. I later interviewed and stayed in that position as Assistant Superintendent for another four years, retiring in 2012.

━ ━

For someone who was, at many turns, dead set against teaching, I had a very enriching career. I was never one to follow protocol, and I know there are things I did that I would not have done today, but at no time did I do something I felt was not for the benefit of the students.

━ ━

As I said, I retired from the San Bernardino City Unified School District in 2003, then retired again from the San Bernardino County Superintendent of Schools Office in 2012. But that hasn't affected my participation in education. I no longer stand in front of a class full of students, I no longer supervise teachers and make sure the school is a safe environment for all, I don't even call parents about absences or tardiness, but I do have a say in what they are taught, accountability of both students and staff, making sure funding is available for a quality education and that students are being prepared for college, work or any other quality of life.

I am now an elected member of the school board.

CHAPTER FIVE
Marriage, Family, and Religion

If marriages are made in heaven, there should be rain checks.
~Margaret Hill

You may be wondering what I was doing all that time I was teaching. You know I was divorced, and, if you know me, you know I am married now, so I may as well tell you how that came to be.

I met my husband Bob at one of our pinochle rendezvous. He was an excellent card player and since my social life for the past nine years had consisted of playing cards or bowling. I wasn't great at either but certainly better at bowling. My neighbor introduced us and I can still remember our first date as he showed up with this funny looking suit on but he had a great sense of humor

My husband, Robert "Bob" Hill.

that he has since lost some of it. We got to be good friends and at some point, decided to get married. Neither can remember the proposal. After a year plus of playing cards, shopping at Fedco, and taking his son to the zoo, we became serious with our relationship. He never did like bowling the way that I did. Most of the time, he would join a league so that I didn't have to go there alone.

Bob and I made several attempts to get married in 1978 and 1979 but it seemed as though it was not meant to be. Every weekend that we were supposed to go to Las Vegas to tie the knot, one of us got ill or had to work, or had a conference. In May of 1979, we said we were going to get married no matter what and had shared our plans for a May 27 wedding. I had just finished packing the previous morning when my niece, Erika, the daughter of my brother Kenneth and his wife, Mamie, called and suggested that we take our cars to her parents' home to wash so ours would be all ready for the trip. I thought it was a good idea since Bob was at work and we still had time on our hands before the departure.

Erika got to her parents' house first, but neither of them were home, nor was their 16-year-old daughter Diana. When I drove up, I saw a strange car in front of the house and then Erika ran to my car with the most shocking words, "Diana is dead."

I couldn't believe it. Diana had recently celebrated her 16th birthday and was an amazing competitive roller skater and lovely young woman. But the strange car belonged to a man from the coroner's office who showed me a picture of Diana, clearly deceased.

Kenneth worked at Norton Air Force Base and Mamie worked in Rialto. Neither had yet been told and we wanted to be the ones to do so, not the coroner. He listened to us quietly and stoically, then suggested we all go to Rialto to tell Mamie, which we did.

In the hours that followed, we learned Diana had recently gotten into trouble at school and was on restriction. She had asked her mom if she could go and get a pizza the previous evening, but instead went off to be with her friends. They were driving near Pacific High School and Diana was sitting in the lap of the front passenger when they got into an accident and she was nearly decapitated.

To me, the earth stood still that day. There was no way I was going to get married. But my brother said, "Please go. Do it for Diana." So we went to Las Vegas and got married. It was a Sunday and, truth be told, I hardly remember the ceremony. I don't even remember signing a marriage license and once, when I needed a copy of it, neither Bob nor I were able to find it. But every year when we celebrate our anniversary, we always remember Diana.

$$\longrightarrow \quad \longleftarrow$$

Another thing people tell me they think about me is that I am religious. I have never figured out why that is.

I have written about growing up Baptist and becoming Catholic, the doctrine I still espouse. In California, I did attend St. Anne's for many years, but once Father O'Toole died, it wasn't the same. I never found another Catholic church that connected with me in the same way.

At one point, I realized I liked Gospel Music and began attending Baptist churches, most often St. Paul's American Methodist Episcopal (AME) Temple Missionary, The Centre, New Hope Missionary and Ecclesia. All in San Bernardino. I liked Bishop Powell, Pastor Beckley, Pastor Campbell and Pastor Turner, and others, as well. When I signed in, I would put my name, but not my church affiliation because I didn't attend one single church. I wondered how long it would be before someone questioned me about that.

A few months later, I was called and asked what church I belonged to.

"I think God is in all of them," I replied.

Thinking about my developing tendency to "church-hop," I remembered my parents each attending different churches, and my attending with both of them. Once, at the Holiness Church, my sister who was very young at the time, jumped up and started shouting, like some of the people. I knew she was faking, but it was still funny. We didn't go there for a while.

Still, every Sunday, I had gone to a church, just not always the same church. There are so many things that become imbedded in your soul at a young age. Later, when I moved to Norfolk, I didn't join a church. I would go to different churches with friends, and that was fine with me. I liked hearing the different sermons, the different perspectives. And as I've written, although I was overly enthusiastic about taking classes to join the Catholic Church because it meant so much to my first husband, I did it.

I knew it was right to go to church, but I never felt a need to attend just one. Even now, I sometimes wake up and think I want to go to St. Paul's today, or maybe to the Baptist Church, or maybe watch a church service on television, or listen to James Cleveland or Andre' Crouch on Pandora before I go to sleep. I also like the prayer meetings held the first Friday of the month at 6 a.m. It's one hour and a different minister delivers the service and the piano player is very good. In no way does that make me believe I have strayed from God.

▶ ◀

My brother-in-law disagrees, saying I should be born again and attend a single church. When I asked him why, he said we should all be reborn in God and tithe. When I responded that I did those things, he had no justification for his linear thinking. I told him when he could justify it, I would pick a church; in the meantime, I would be both giving and forgiving.

Eventually, he stopped asking me.

I feel I am living the will of God without being re-baptized or going to a single church on a regular basis. My husband teases me that I go to so many churches with various reverends, saying, I never knew of anyone who knew so many ministers without getting hooked!"

I have to say that although I do know many clergy, I am a little angry with churches these days. They could be out in the community more. When I see a church closed all week that disappoints me. Of course, I suppose I could do more there, too. Fact is, I have never been an active person in church. I've never sat on a Deacon Board. I have done church services, though.

Ready for another busy day.

The first time was at Reverend Powell's church, The Centre at Highland. They were located on Palm near Pacific. I was the speaker for the graduation, but I didn't talk about the Bible. Honestly, I cannot tell you where to find a single verse. Instead, I talked about attitudes and behaviors, and I spoke about life-changing ministries. I don't know about you, but for me, that demonstrated God in the lives of those new graduates.

CHAPTER SIX
Leadership has its Challenges

Remember to always be on your best behavior as
your worst enemy might be watching.
~Margaret Hill

San Bernardino County Schools is the public entity that oversees the budgets for the thirty-three districts in the county. I went to County Schools at the request of Dr. Herb Fischer who was the superintendent at that time. We had a previous working relationship at San Bernardino High School where he was the principal and I was one of his vice principals. He was also my mentor.

He asked me if I would be willing to serve as his Assistant Superintendent and I said I'd be honored. He was pleased to hear that and said he'd start the wheels into motion, but would not make the announcement until he notified the school board. Shortly, though, he called a meeting of all the classified and certificated staff of the Administrative Division. The Assistant Superintendent retired at the end of June and I was appointed interim July 1, 2006. I was a little nervous because I could only assume one of the veterans in that division would be interested and perhaps hoping to get the call that I got. Dr. Fischer announced my appointment as Interim Assistant Superintendent.

Then he walked out of the room.

No one said anything, initially, least of all me. I had no idea he was going to announce my appointment in that way. But then I knew I needed to rally, so I squared my shoulders and addressed the group.

"You know me and I'm a good listener," I began. "I'm not going to demand much, but I do want to demand something now."

They all just looked at me.

I smiled and asked, "When is the next potluck?"

Everyone laughed and the ice was broken, thus beginning my six years as Assistant Superintendent for Administrative Services.

—▶ ◀—

But I surmised it wasn't going to be an immediately smooth transition, and I was correct. Shortly thereafter, I began to hear grumbling about who should have gotten the position but I had learned from the best and felt together we could work as a team. I knew I did not want enemies and there were people who could make my position difficult so I empowered as many staff members as I could.

—▶ ◀—

There were challenges that I thought I would not have to deal with but the staff members did not get along with each other. My office was located across from Human Resources and that was a blessing because I had staff members who beat a path reporting on one another almost on a daily basis. The Interim Assistant Superintendent in that division realized there were problems, so they brought in a consultant from Palm Springs to conduct some team building exercises. Those weren't particularly effective and word kept getting back to me about the things people would say.

My office covered child welfare & attendance, the homeless, foster youth, nursing services, nutrition and health, so I was always in the community securing resources or visiting districts to ensure things were moving smoothly. Barstow, Baker, Trona; I went all over. I guess people must have thought I was out running around not being very resourceful to the 33 districts because when I retired, I was concerned when they didn't replace me. I initially thought it was a matter of budget cuts, yet all the other departments had directors except for mine. I had to do all the attendance reviews, as well as employee evaluations and disciplining with no assistance.

When I left, I was told that the work I was doing was going to be absorbed by two departments. Once that happened, and the full volume or work was realized, people were amazed at how much we got completed. I guess initially they weren't aware I was also working nights and weekends.

Recently, I ran into someone I worked with at County Schools who said she was amazed at the negative things one of my staff members had said about me.

"I thought we had a pretty good group when you left, but later I realized what kind of backstabbing was really going on," she said.

But I knew I had made a positive impact for the students and although it wasn't the work environment I'd have chosen, I know good things were done. When I go to School Board meetings now, people still tell me they appreciated my work and all I did that was outside the box for County Schools, such as taking food to foster kids and advocating for the county and its employees and students.

If I made a mistake, it was in trusting my co-workers too much. I had amazing and very knowledgeable people working for me and I cared for them dearly; however, these next two incidents were my prize excuse-ers. Once, one told me she had to attend a workshop in Ontario. I happened to be at the same venue for another event and thought I'd pop in to tell her hello, but when I arrived, there was no event and no one there knew anything about it. When I returned to the office later in the day she was there.

"I looked for you at the workshop," I said.

"I was there," she replied defensively. "You must have missed me."

Another time, an employee said she couldn't come in because she was at jury duty and her group was being held for the rest of the day and she was on break. But the person who relayed the message said she could hear the sounds of the dog barking and realized the person was at home, not at the courthouse.

Clearly, it was an interesting group.

They would regularly tattle on each other. But when someone would ask what I was going to do, they'd say "She can't do anything." A few of them presented challenges quite often. Still, they were kind when I found I had breast cancer and needed to take time off to recover from surgery, and they were kind when I returned.

As I had scheduled my cancer surgery in November, some of the staff said they wanted to take me out for my December birthday beforehand. They took me to a local grill called BJ's and while we were there, one of the attendees – a fellow from Valley College – took our picture. A few weeks later, the same photo appeared in the County school's newsletter.

The Superintendent called me into his office.

"What is wrong with this picture?" he asked.

"I don't know," I replied honestly.

He went on to point out that the picture had been taken in front of BJ's bar and now over 10,000 people saw County Schools' staff standing in front of alcohol bottles. I saw his point, but also noted none of us had been drinking, and no one was photographed with even a water glass in their hands.

───▶ ◀───

It was that kind of thing that consistently got me in trouble. One day, a friend asked me to go to lunch with her because she was having a bad day and wanted a change of scenery and a listening ear. I, of course, complied.

She wanted to go to the buffet at the San Manuel Casino which was located not far from the office. On our lunch hour, we decided to play the slots instead of having lunch. As luck would have it, I hit a jackpot and the young lady who arrived with my winnings was the niece of a co-worker. I knew I was doing nothing wrong, but asked her to keep the winnings quiet. Still, somehow word got out and, once again, I was the receiver of self-righteous wrath.

The smile on a winner's face

Overall, the six years I spent there were good ones because of the value of the work we did for the schools. When I retired, I didn't fail to mention my transgressions in my parting speech; no use in giving people something to talk about that I didn't say first.

➤ ◄—

When the Superintendent, Dr. Thomas, was entrusted with introducing me at as then-63rd District Assemblyman Morrell's Woman of the Year, I was a little concerned about what he would say about me. I was surprised when he recognized the community work I had done. He noted I had served on policy councils with all the county agencies and noted the importance of that effort. I was so surprised, I almost had to laugh but it was indeed an honor to hear the respect he had for what I had done for six years.

I came to the school board because I was angry over some of the same pettiness.

There were three consultant groups asked to submit a proposal to select the next superintendent for the San Bernardino City Unified School District and we were number three.

The Board President started our interview with an awkward question.

"How many minorities have you hired as superintendents?"

I knew the answer was zero, because the only vacancies were in three cities that were scarcely populated. But the leader of our team stated he did not know.

Then a County School Board Member asserted I shouldn't even be on the team since I was also on the Board of a charter schools and that I worked for the county.

I was angry, but determined not to show it.

"I have been in the community for 40 years and can think for myself. I am ethical and fair. But take me off the committee if it is that bothersome to you," I said.

I was honest, but minds were made up before I spoke. County Schools received zero votes. An outside firm was brought in, and I am still ticked.

In July, I was at a sorority event in New Orleans when Bob called to tell me I needed to call City Schools because they wanted my input in the selection of the new superintendent. I told him it would be a cold day in you-know-where before I would do anything for them again. Then in August, Dr. Thomas received a letter requesting his support in the selection process. He sent me the letter with a note attached to see him. I went to see Dr. Thomas and for the first time since he became superintendent, I knew he was going to give me the assignment that I did not want.

"I hope you're not going to do what I think you're going to do," I said. But he acknowledged the need was significant and my help considered very beneficial. I acquiesced, reminding him it was because he had asked me, not because I wanted to.

But when we walked into the room, the consultants were there meeting with another participant. The door had been closed, so we apologized and introduced ourselves only to find we weren't on the list of attendees. I was so embarrassed. The other participant graciously shared his time and we spoke, then left. I had walked most of the way to my car when I felt the need to go back and confront Brenda, the staff assistant that I told I would be there at the stated appointment time.

"Didn't I talk to you when I confirmed for the meeting?" I asked.

"You did," she said, adding, "I gave your RSVP to the board secretary.

I asked if I had RSVP'd why I was not on the list. She said she had turned the information in. I asked who else had access to appointments, and she said it was just Jennifer. I didn't stay to see Jennifer because I knew she would only have done as directed.

I was so angry.

I went home and told Bob about it.

"Don't you think it's time you run for the School Board?" he asked.

The next morning, I shared with my staff what happened the previous day. Sherman said he thought it was time for me to throw my hat in the ring to become a school board member. I smiled but said little. Later, Eric, the director of a non-profit tutorial program had called me about another matter and before we signed off, I mentioned I was thinking of running.

"You've got to do it," he said emphatically.

Five minutes later, he called me back.

"The filing period closes today. You have to get your paper-work in by five," he said.

I called a few more people and all agreed with Eric, Sherman and my husband, so I went to the registrar and filled out my paperwork. I didn't have a candidate statement or anything, just my basic paperwork, but it was filed on time.

When I got home from work, I went to my Facebook and posted, "I did something today I didn't think I would. I went to the registrar of voters and filed paperwork for the school board." Then I closed it down and didn't look at the site until around midnight.

There were 98 posts, most from former students who said "You have to run" and gave me reasons why. That confirmed to me that I had done the right thing.

With the wheels in motion, I realized that I needed a cam-paign manager, and so I asked about five people but no one would do it. Then I called my niece, Erika, and asked her and she said, "Auntie Margaret, I barely vote!"

So then I called Terrance, my vice chair for the Gangs & Drugs Task Force. He calls me Mom and I know I can trust him, but he said he'd never done anything like that before, but he would give it a try with help.

So I called Erika back and asked if she'd do it with Terrance's help, and she agreed.

If you're a voter in the County of San Bernardino, you may have received a phone call on my behalf. Know that it was like from a youth in trouble volunteering for service hours.

It was so funny. I'd walk into the phone room and they would all be as polite as they could be... but they didn't know who I was. One day, Erika brought this to my attention.

"The kids are making calls for you, but they don't know who you are."

So I asked my friend Denise to accompany me to the office where these young people were making calls on my behalf so I could meet with them. When we walked in, though, everyone congratulated Denise. I guess it always has to be the White woman. I quickly introduced myself and they were so embarrassed, but we all laughed about it. I made calls, also. I wanted them to see I could work alongside them and that I knew how hard they were working.

They did a great job of organizing and doing fundraisers. Either Terrance, Monica (another volunteer) or Erika was always with me when I went to speak. I enjoyed speaking, too. I became more and more assured of my speaking skills as I talked about the issues that concerned me. I was speaking the truth and, through that, I found my voice for the community.

But that voice was squelched when I went to do a book signing during the campaign. I actually didn't see that it would be a problem at the time, but the signing - scheduled at San Andreas High School – was abruptly cancelled because I was a candidate. After that, we were more careful, but even when I was at school events, some people wouldn't introduce me. Still, I was endorsed by all the unions and I'd go all over and people said they were voting for me.

But knowing a lot of people and getting a lot of votes are two different things.

The night of the election, I was at Mardi Gras restaurant for my campaign celebration and Eric was at his computer.

"Quiet everybody," he said. "The first results are in," he said.

I felt the butterflies start to fly all over my stomach.

"I'm going to start at the top and go down," he began.

I held my breath.

"Margaret Hill, 4,600 votes. Lynda, a little over 2,000 votes," he said.

I knew I had a place and I jumped for joy!

I ended up around 14,000 votes. Lynda had about 11,000. No one was close to us.

I have thoroughly enjoyed being on the board. Linda is about the arts. I'm about attendance. It has been a way to give back to many students, and that does my heart good. But there have also been some surprises as to what my expectations are as a board member, such as the number of unscheduled board meetings and workshops.

CHAPTER SEVEN

Learning for Life, Teaching for Life

You never know if you're last until you run the race.
~Margaret Hill

I suppose I could be called a lifelong learner. I believe that is what has both kept me sharp and given me the mental energy to keep moving forward these many years.

As a Norfolk State undergrad, I also took some classes at Old Dominion and through the University of Virginia extension program. Later, when I came to California, I took classes at Cal State, as well as a few non-transferrable courses at University of California at Riverside.

But it was one cold and rainy night in December of 1980, as I walked from the student parking lot of California State University to the Pfau Library that I decided not all of my learning should be confined to a classroom. I started think how I'd been attending school for 35 years and decided to give myself a break, so after I completed my classes for my Masters in Education and Administrative Credential, I simply went home and I've never been back.

So how do I call myself a lifelong learner?

I think that comes through applying what I have been taught in the classroom to the observations I make about life… and to the research I do for my books and presentations… and to occasional forays into higher education. For instance, I once realized that it would be a good idea to learn Spanish so I signed up for a class at San Bernardino Valley College. I was excited to go and felt the new skill would make me better prepared to work with people who did not speak English. I quickly learned I had no ability to pronounce the words thus dashing my hopes to better communicate. I attended four classes, then dropped the course. Later, former San Bernardino Mayor – an amazing Spanish teacher herself – Judith Valles taught me how to pronounce the vowels. I believe if she'd been my Spanish teacher, I'd probably be able to speak it today.

I also took golf lessons, but I can't say I was LPGA material either.

Another way in which I make learning a part of my everyday life is to stay a part of the local environment. I have written about my election to the School Board, but there was – and is – more. Since my college days, I have always been involved with my community in one way or another.

When I was in Virginia, I belonged to a horticultural club. That instilled in me a love of gardening and I am proud of the beautiful, healthy vegetables I grow today.

When I came to California, I joined Delta Sigma Theta Sorority as a graduate student. We would meet on Sundays at 2 p.m., which worked well because it followed church and a social lunch. This sorority was founded on January 13, 1913 by 22 collegiate women at Howard University, a historically black college, to promote academic excellence and provide assistance to those in need. Since its founding, more than 200,000 predominantly black, college educated women have joined the organization. There are currently more than 1,000 collegiate and alumnae chapters located in the United States and throughout the world.

In 1981, a group of us were approached by one of the Los Angeles chapters to charter The National Sorority of Phi Delta Kappa, Inc. I am proud to be one of the charter members and our chapter is Delta Rho. This sorority emerged from a dream of teachers from New Jersey to establish a sorority to promote sisterhood among teachers and to uphold the highest ideas of the teaching profession. The sorority was officially incorporated on May 23, 1923.

The National Sorority of Phi Delta Kappa, Inc., Delta Rho Chapter.

When I started working at San Bernardino High School in 1985, I got involved with the Black Culture Foundation. It happened kind of serendipitously, in fact. I had been trying to get home from a Saturday event and got stuck behind their annual parade. I complained about it to someone who happened to be involved with the organization, and they put me on the committee. I guess that was my punishment for complaining. This is a non-profit organization, run solely by volunteers. For over forty years, this organization has given scholarships to youth in our community to help with their college expenses. During that time, they have also sponsored the Black History Parade, the crowning of the Senior (age 55+) King and Queen, the Black Rose Awards for un-sung heroes in our community, and the Miss Black San Bernardino pageant.

Also while at San Andreas High School, I was asked to be on the first YMCA Board for the newly forming Highland branch which was located in the old Crowell Building on Palm Avenue. I had been on the San Bernardino YMCA Board in the 1970s, and I guess people thought my knowledge of the history of the organization would be helpful. Later, we went to a building next to the old police facility on Base Line, but it was very small. The city finally built the Central Avenue facility where today's YMCA stands and provides recreation services to the people of Highland. As Highland is a contract city with no recreation services of their own, this really is the only place residents are provided access to low-cost recreation services outside of the schools.

A few years later, a group of us got together to see what we could do to help parolees get back on their feet. I was working for Dr. Herb Fischer at the time and while he saw the need for such a program to make parolees successful, he didn't think it was a program that we could contribute to since we are in the business of educating our youth.

"Margaret, you're not going to do it," he told me one day when I'd explained what we were thinking.

But I told him no one else wanted to be the lead agent for the program, and I talked about how we should be involved because many of the parolees are the fathers of the students in our schools. We were working with a group of people who truly cared, and we knew we would be able to make a difference. The CREST Program, as it was called at its inception, now has reporting centers in Moreno Valley, Victorville and San Bernardino as of this writing. I think our compassion made the difference.

In CREST/CSRI, while the staff provided administration and guidance, they put the parolees in charge of pretty much everything else. They keep the place clean, conducted orientations with new people, cooked and served the food for the annual celebration/recognition event, and enforced the rules. Those rules included no profanity, no gang clothing or throwing of gang signs or other types of gang behavior. New people are told, "If you want to be a man, you can join us." And they're told that by people like themselves. We just set the wheels in motion and kept them running administratively.

The idea belonged to Dr. Carolyn Eggleston from Cal State San Bernardino. She got the men to organize and form a cohesive team. We brought it to the attention of the mayor who donated neckties for the men, and to Nordstrom which donated 60 suits when we got started. The men clean up, dress up, and man up for interviews with security firms and Caltrans. Last year, one man who had been in prison for 20 years had us all in tears when he talked about how much the job he got with the city of San Bernardino meant to him.

The current recidivism rate for the program is about 16-percent, much less than for many other programs. I believe it has stayed successful because the men have made the decisions in a responsible manner which, for some of them, was a lifetime first.

――▶ ◀――

I've stayed involved in the organizations I believe do the most good for the community, so my time makes an impact.

I have worked a lifetime to build a reputation as a trustworthy person of character in my community. I am also proud of the fact that just about everything I've decided to do has been because I was asked.

Of course, there was a group or two that I chose not to join, as well.

$$\longrightarrow \longleftarrow$$

In addition to groups organized by and with others, I began my own organization – the Maggie's Kids Foundation – to meet a need that was particularly close to my heart. Proceeds from this and my previous book go there, so I want to tell you about it.

As I've written, in July of 1987 when I was hired as Principal of San Andreas High School, I was more than a little concerned. I knew this was where students who couldn't meet traditional high school expectations were, more or less, warehoused, and I had never heard a single success story about a one of them. As a matter of fact, I remember thinking, 'Oh, no! That's where I've been sending all the students who had given me grief!'

Of course, it didn't take me long to fall in love with the place and the people there. While the students had major challenges, they were each real people with the potential to be wonderful citizens. Some had learning disabilities, some had extremely limited resources at home, or drug-addicted parents. Some had the responsibility of raising siblings or their own children. Many were homeless.

I realized these students had been swept aside for the students who wanted to get an education without disruption, and that is okay. We simply needed to provide a place where they would work through pain those other students never realized so we could eventually send them out into the world with the ability to create positive lives.

It was the homeless students who most uniquely touched my heart. Each year, I must have encountered at least 20 young people who didn't know where they would sleep that night or where they would get their next meal once school closed for the day.

I remember one Monday morning that a young man that I will call Don walked into my office.

"Mrs. Hill, I need to talk to you," he said.

I offered him a seat and he immediately began: "You'll never guess what happened to me."

He explained that he had secured his mother's okay to spend the weekend with a friend the Friday past, but when he got home to prepare for school Monday morning, he found a note saying she'd moved to New York and he was on his own.

What do you say to a child who has been put in a position like that? Well, in this case, the student stayed in his friend's home until his mother returned to get him.

Another child I remember was a boy who always wore a long trench coat. The look was unusual and, frankly, concerned me because I thought he might be hiding and selling drugs in that big coat. I shared my concerns with the School Police who conducted a "random" check focusing on this young man.

But when they searched him, all they found was a cell phone. It was confiscated and given to me, and he was sent to my office.

"Why are you bringing a cell phone to school when you know I is against the rules," I asked.

"I have to have that phone in case my boss calls," he said. "He gave me that phone so that he can call me to work when there is an emergency."

"So why don't you leave the phone at home until school is out like everyone else has to?" I asked.

"I don't have a home," he replied.

I believed him, but felt it must be because he chose not to live with his parents, so I asked how I could get in touch with his parents. Then he explained he hadn't heard from his parents in over a year and that everything he owned, he kept on his back, washing his clothes at night.

These were regular kids in bad situations. I knew I had to do something to help them. So when I prepared to retire, I decided I would make it known that instead of proclamations and going-away gifts, I'd like donations to be made to build the legacy needed to start Maggie's Kids. People listened, and when I took my leave of San Andreas, the Foundation was officially born. The community and staff supported my vision and gave unselfishly, and, as I said, book proceeds go there as well.

You may wonder why I named it Maggie's Kids when I never go by that name myself. The reason is a tribute to the students who were involved in the San Andreas Entrepreneurship Program and opened a café at the District's Administration Annex which they chose to name after me. But they felt the name Margaret was not sporty enough, so they changed it to Maggie.

I like to hope when people see the name of the Foundation, they think of the drive and ability each of those "forgotten" kids was demonstrating through their work.

Even more so, I'd like to hope that inspiration results in a level of funding that can provide a dormitory or alumni house for homeless students.

CHAPTER EIGHT

My Cancer Journey

*Never stop dreaming because your worst
nightmare might come true.
~Margaret Hill*

I can look back now and see that as I grew from a shy little girl with low self-esteem to a strong and positive woman, it was how I dealt with the combination of good and not-so-good that has done the most to shape me. I have always felt that the greatest strength a person can develop is their ability to respond to situations.

For me, that ability was significantly tested in August of 2009 when I went to see my doctor.

➤ ◀

I went there for medical reasons since I was developing problems with my feet.

I have always been concerned about the health of my feet. As a woman of limited height, I have always favored the advantage available in wearing high heels. My doctor had told me flats were better for me, so I got some and kept them in the car. And, of course, after a while, my feet got more and more sore so that eventually I found it difficult to walk without pain.

I had a trip to Peru planned and knew it would involve a great deal of walking which could be made impossible if he wanted to do surgery, so I bought some travel-ready flat shoes and informed the doctor I would make an appointment but I did not state I would do so when I returned in October from my international vacation.

Peru was lovely, but my feet were more uncomfortable than ever when I got home, so making that long-delayed doctor visit was high on my priority list. But when I called, I encountered problems with my insurance since I failed to identify the plan. Benefits automatically assigned me a different plan, which meant I had to go to a new physician at a new hospital.

➤ ◄

My new young doctor was named Dr. Wu and he was a general practitioner at Loma Linda University Hospital. He looked to me to be about 16-years-old, but he was thorough and asked questions which I appreciated.

After my examination, he said he was concerned about a lump he'd noticed in my breast and suggested I get a mammogram. I had had one performed a year previous, but made the appointment anyway. That led to a sonogram, then a meeting with a nurse who informed me I had cancer and asked me to wait to see the doctor.

"It's bad news that you have cancer, but good news that the type you have is the easiest to treat and to cure," she told me.

I went home and shared the news with Bob, who became very quiet. We talked about his concerns and he shared how he did not deal with illness comfortably, and when his father was very ill and on life-support at the hospital the nurse told the family only one person at a time could be in the room with him. Bob said he was out the door before she finished talking. He didn't like hospitals, and I knew he was not going to be the right person for me to ask for help when I was there.

➤ ◀

I was Assistant Superintendent of County Schools at the time of my diagnosis. I have written about how I had a few staff members that created a dysfunctional work environment, but I also noted the people there were very kind to me during my medical issues.

I scheduled my surgery for November 8, 2010, and a leave of absence from November through January. My boss told me to take off as much time as I needed, but once I was cleared to return, I was ready. I had been working for 50 years at the time and had never taken off work except for a four-week hysterectomy recovery period and these two months.

I approached my diagnosis the way I have approached most of the challenges in my life. I collected the information I needed, then proceeded through each phase. I remember my sister, Clasteen, asking me if I'd cried when I heard the diagnosis, and I asked her why would I. I knew I was in good hands and so I was not worried or panicked. I simply knew what I needed to do, and I did it.

I also didn't keep it from myself. After I told Bob, I told my boss, then my employees and my family and my bowling group. If someone said they'd heard I was going to need surgery, I said I was. I didn't want pity, but I also didn't want to hide such a major life change. I didn't see it as a particularly unusual situation; it was something that was happening. I have always been able to name two or three people going through whatever challenge I am also facing, and this was no different. Some people get mean when they are diagnosed. Or they try and blame someone. For me, it was just a thing I faced, and I tried to be kind to people when they felt uncomfortable around me because I was sick. They'd say, "I can't believe how healthy you look." One even asked me if I really had cancer.

I faced it as I've faced everything else in my life: pragmatically and with the understanding that an ultimate good might be gained. I even gave myself a pre-surgery trip to Key West, Florida.

Perhaps somewhere in my subconscious, I knew it was a possibility, so that prepared me more than others may have been.

I haven't talked about it before, but it makes sense to bring it up here. That is, my mother had only one breast. That was something I took for granted growing up. I knew she had undergone surgery, but it was nothing we talked about; back then, you never spoke about such things. My father died of lung cancer, and when I was 26, my mother died, as well. At the time of my surgery, my brother was in remission from prostate cancer.

From June through September, I went to chemotherapy. I scheduled Fridays off initially, but I was never sick from the treatments, so I would just get my treatment and go back to work. My friend Denise Lundy – who didn't share my husband's aversion to hospitals - would take me to my appointments. Once following the remodeling of the hospital by the very generous George and Pauline Murillo of the San Manuel Tribe, I was asked to be a part of a film documenting the contributions that the Murillo's made to

At the Believe Walk about a month before my cancer surgery.

the Cancer Center. Denise shared I had many TV and radio interviews when the film maker said I was the best interviewee. I like to think I'm a natural.

My surgery took place as scheduled and went smoothly. I began radiation the last of that December through the first part of February, 2011.

Administering radiation is an interesting process. The medical team suits up as if they are going into space, and the patient is forced to stay perfectly still in horribly uncomfortable positions throughout the procedure. Once, the computer was acting up and I had to stay in the same position for nearly 15 minutes. I seriously thought I was going to cry, and it takes a lot for that to happen. Other than that, I had no issues with radiation. People tell you it's a possibility, but for me, other than the contortions, it was not at all painful.

I learned a number of things from having cancer.

The first is that you should get regular check-ups and that you shouldn't wait to see the doctor if you suspect a problem. I know other things in life get in the way, but those other things won't be possible at all if you're gone. If I had waited much longer to go in for my feet, I'd probably found out about my cancer too late and would be pushing up daisies now.

Another thing I learned is to follow the advice your doctor gives you, and do so to the letter. I was told not to lift things and to wear my compression sleeve to reduce the possibility of lymphedema. I did lift, and I didn't wear the sleeve, and now I have a heavy and continually swollen arm that requires a great deal of massage. Today, I sleep with my arms wrapped and elevated, then wear long sleeves year-round.

It is annoying and bothersome, even though it has allowed me to make some new wardrobe purchases. I would not have had to deal with such things if I had followed the advice I was given; but then again, if it is the worst thing I have to deal with, I feel blessed.

And that leads me to the most important thing I have learned from my journey with cancer: life is precious and every day is important. Those are simple thoughts and I am sure they are said every day by people who have no idea what they truly mean, but I can tell you they are true. Cherish every day of your life. I do.

In October of 2012, in honor of Breast Cancer Month, I even wrote a poem about the experience. I entitled it "My Trip Down Breast Cancer Lane, or 'Yes, they are false; my real ones tried to kill me." It goes like this:

I am one of six children
Who were born and raised on a farm,
We all had different interests and abilities
That did not cause any harm.

All three of my brothers served in the military
Leisurely two enjoy golfing while one was a mechanic,
My two sisters could knit, crochet, sing and dance
But I was the one who always panicked.

Both of my parents died from cancer
I'm not sure about my mother but my dad loved to smoke
I've made fun of a lot of things in life
But this cancer just isn't a joke.

As someone who was diagnosed with this same deadly disease
My words to my God Almighty was and is "thank you please."
I appreciate you listening to me tell my story
So sit back, relax and take a mental note,
I will give as many details as I possibly remember
And apologize for not memorizing everything that I wrote.

Insurance benefits have a limited window of time
For one to make changes in person or on line.
Now I had not made a change in over five years
So for my husband and me, I had no fears.

It started when I went to my doctor and
complained about my feet
He told me there are things we must do,
A referral to the podiatrist was recommended
But I had a recommendation too.

You see, a vacation had been planned for Peru
A place I had never gone,
I wasn't going to let my three friends taking this trip
And leave me home all alone.

When I returned from my vacation I visited my doctor
Who wondered where I went,
Through frustration he said this has been delayed far too long
And offered to make me a podiatrist appointment.
I got a telephone call the very next day
Telling me that my insurance had been changed,
Benefits provided me HMO and cancelled my PPO
So other plans I had to arrange.

January 2010 I had an appointment with my new doctor
Who checked my vitals and gave me a full body exam,
He was concerned with what he felt in my breast
And quickly recommended a mammogram.

Being obedient I scheduled an appointment
Since I hadn't had a mammogram for over a year,
I was more than surprised when I got a call from Loma Linda
Saying don't delay, you need to get in here.

During self-examination, I noticed a change in my left breast
But never did I fret,
I blamed it on having poor nutritional habits
And to be honest, I just considered it fat.

By June I had my first chemo treatment
It was not as devastating as I thought it would be,
The cancer center staff was very accommodating
And the valet parking was free.
By September I had my last chemo treatment
And was told surgery would be scheduled more or less,
They frowned when the date they scheduled was not good
But I told them I was going on vacation to Key West.

November 8 was the day my doctor and I agreed
To have this operation to save my life,
A radical mastectomy was scheduled for 7 a.m.
And I could tell that my husband feared for his wife.

The operation, I was told, was very successful
And that in itself was a relief,
I was discharged from the hospital the very next day
My stay in that beautiful facility was very brief.

Radiation treatments began in late December
Wow! What a great way to bring in a new year,
With all the prayers, visits, food and flowers I received
That took away most of my fear.

February was the month for my last radiation treatment
And these treatments left their mark,
While the worst part of those visits were being strapped down
And having parts of my body very dark.

Now is the time for the real extreme makeover
Certainly, I had decisions to make,
Will I consider breast reconstruction surgery?
Or the rest of my life wear the fake?

Another decision on my plate to consider
Was what to do about my lack of hair?
It had gotten so easy to shampoo in the shower whenever
Then leave the house without one care.

I know I am truly blessed as many others are
And I pray for the families of those who were not so blessed,
I thank my God for giving me another chance
By letting me pass this cancer test.

I will not take anything for granted again
Because in this world we all have a price to pay,
Always do what is good for everyone walking on this earth
If in this world we plan to stay.

Since I'm not doing this for any type of recognition
Don't remember me for cancer but the deeds I have done,
God used me to show others that cancer
is not the end of the world
So be kind and respectful to your family,
friends and enemies – just have fun.

CHAPTER NINE
Life Guidance

Why are some people as beautiful as roses
while others are damaging as thorns?
~Margaret Hill

People who know me today know an evolved Margaret who has been uniquely shaped by the journey of her years. Few know that when I was small, I was painfully shy, crying if I was asked to read aloud in class and running to my older sister for protection when I was afraid. Few know about the Margaret who dreamed of being a teacher or nurse out of an innate compassion, but lacked the confidence needed to build relationships.

The stylish woman my friends and colleagues know today would be hard pressed to visualize the little girl in braids with jeans and tennis shoes who spent her high school years trying to fade into the background so as not to be compared to a lovely older sister or clever brother. And my students would certainly not recognize the girl who put off doing her homework or struggled through class after class.

I have learned to be bold through adversity, and patient through the development of a lifetime of strengths. I cherish my patience, not only because of its origins, but because I now recognize that it is the pathway to an untroubled life.

I have learned to be curious through considered observation and, in turn, blessed to develop the ability to read people. This has made me an effective orator who, I believe, has been placed in front of groups of others who are intended to benefit from my words. Sometimes, that comes in the form of speeches before school or community groups, and sometimes, it is in the written word.

If you have benefitted from the latter, I hope you will also consider the following advice I offer because it has long weighed heavy on my mind and will likely be the next of my life adventures.

Here's what I'd like to do.

Increased parent involvement: I would most like to come up with a magic way of fixing parents. I wish I could so they would understand and be able to work with the schools. We need to teach parenting skills because we know parents want the best for their children.

I was so excited recently to have gone to a school in San Bernardino and the principal said, "Students here want to learn how to sew, so now we're going to make it possible for them." Can you imagine the implications of this? It's what San Bernardino City School District Superintendent Dale Marsden calls "Cradle to Career" education. It doesn't mean our students will all be manual laborers, but it means they will all learn job skills, both technical skills and those soft skills like showing up on time, answering responsibly to your boss, etc. I think there are great opportunities here.

I've been thinking of writing a brief but practical book that can go into hospital waiting rooms. On the outside would be something like "A Life Guide," and you could push a lever in the cover that would address the basics as children get older. Just the basics, but basics anyone could hold in their hands.

——→ ←——

We also need parents to stop waiting for the schools to raise their children. If you can teach a little one before they start school, they will be ready to learn more when they do. Successful people have most often had parents who worked with them when they were small. Kids ask good questions then; they're still honest and they're still inquisitive.

I remember a community meeting consisting of community representatives, school personnel, parents and students that we held at Indian Springs High School on bullying. But it was high school! Why should this have to be done in high school when parents and teachers and others should be talking about how to communicate without bullying long before that?

Parents need to have pointed conversations with their kids. Don't just ask how school was today. Ask what did you learn in science? What did your teacher talk about in social studies? What type of math are you doing and why is it important? Open the lines of communication early and they will stay open for a lifetime.

At San Andreas, I told the students at orientation, "I can't help you once you get into trouble but I can help you before you do." I told them they could tell me anything, and they did, and it made a difference. If they came in and told me I'm having a problem with so- and-so, I'd ask them where were they going to be at break time and then I'd watch and ask the kids they'd fingered relating that to what I saw, not what someone had told me.

I knew so much about what was going on because I made my-self a trustworthy source. Students would come to my office and when they left I'd walk them out talking about their assignments so no one would know what they'd actually been there for. Even with dangerous things, I tried to be there because I knew it was for their benefit.

Once there was a girl who was considered by other students to be one not to approach in a negative way and someone came to me and said she had a gun. It happened to be the same day the SMASH Unit was on campus, so I told an officer and we went to the classroom to do a random search. When it was found she didn't have a gun at all, she simply said, "That's all right. I understand." I called the girl's mother and told her what happened too and she also said she understood. Knowing this girl she probably said something to somebody about having a gun, but it has always bothered me.

Youth & Young Adults' Engagement. Another thing I'd truly like to do is to find a way to communicate with the 18-25 year olds who have just lost their way. But I think that the greatest need is for getting information into the hands of the young mothers.

I would make blue books and the pink books small enough to be easily reproduced and given out… something you could just put in your purse to have when you needed it. Maybe something with keepsake value where you could write things, or check them off.

Families have to instill a culture of learning. Grandmas weren't just designed to be babysitters, they must be considered sources of information and they must freely offer information to new mothers and fathers. You have to ask, 'What did you do when I was small?" "What would you have done differently?"

I always felt if I had a child I would know what to do.

Although I never had one of my own, I raised my brother's son from the time he was a few days old until the year when I left for college. The only reason I knew what to do is that my mom was there to assist me. I had a support system. I remember my mom yelling, "Don't give that baby a bottle lying down. You hold him when you feed him."

Someone needs to tell new parents not to be afraid to seek guidance, that it's not a bad thing, and that it's the thing you should do if you want to do the best you can for your child.

Parents need to know how very smart their children are from the moment they come into the world. Those first three years set the tone for everything a person will be. Kids learn and they remember so much more than we give them credit for. A lot of people say two and three year olds are just babies, but that's not true. They have a brain and a personality and they are forming the adult they will be in those first years.

I'd also say look at the long range plan. You want to be sure when your child is an adult, that they are healthy so you start healthy eating habits early. If you give them fries and chips each day, how can their bodies grow to be healthy adults?

I'd also say always talk to your child from the time it is in the womb. Start that conversation so it's natural when they begin to speak with you. Read to them. Listen to music. Maintain a safe environment without a lot of loud music and profanity which is negative because they will pick up negative habits from that. Create a clean environment that is healthy and pleasant, but make it a social environment.

There are so many things we can do with our kids so that they won't grow up badly and make poor decisions. I still remember a woman who had a four-year-old who wore a big "R" on a chain around his neck and used a "street name." I asked her if she thought that might confuse him. She didn't think so. I sometimes wonder where that child is now.

When I was at San Andreas, I would request from the PAL (Provisional Accelerated Learning) Center their mobile unit which was the reality show for most of our students. On display in it were photos of bullet wounds, venereal diseases, etc. The kids would only go into there once. They saw and they learned. But classes should be offered all the time, parenting classes, too. I honestly think girls would come to those classes even if it wasn't part of their curriculum.

And the boys, too. Someone needs to tell them about

consequences and to value the child, as well as other adult things like child support, and the effect of divorce and separation on children. The guys walk away like it's not my problem. And the girls don't know how to make it the guy's problem. They say I don't want that boy around my child, but they fail to realize that they don't have that option. I ask 'What if you didn't know your dad? How would that make you feel?"

Mostly, I just wish people would think more about others.

That may be an old fashioned perspective, but it's worked for me so far, and I guess we both can agree that it's carried you through to the end of this book. Well, almost.

CHAPTER TEN
When All is Said and Done

(Sometimes you have to do strange things)

Mosquito bites are like candy. Too many bites can make you miserable.
~Margaret Hill

I have been to several funerals in my lifetime. Some lasted as little as fifteen minutes and others as long as three hours. I can certainly appreciate those families who feel bringing closure to the deceased should not have a time limit but the longer it takes to say goodbye results in someone thinking about the bad things you did in life. I'm sure we can all come up with one thing we never want said at our funeral.

Perhaps I am being too optimistic but I feel when I pass away, and once my obituary appears in the local newspapers, the school district's board report, and perhaps mentioned at the City Council meetings in San Bernardino and Highland, I will have an overwhelming crowd at my funeral. This is not a good time to disappoint me. For that reason, I am writing my homegoing services so that all of you will have more time to shop for a nice outfit.

The reason I am writing my own service is two-fold: I know me better than anyone else and I believe funerals should be scheduled to last forty-five minutes and even if you have a minister who likes to speak to those who can still hear him or her, it is okay to allow another fifteen minutes. Pastors Joshua Beckley, Raymond Turner, Larry Campbell, Sam Casey, Jason Evans, Ray Miller, Phillip Powell, Jim James and Rabbi Hillel Cohn are all ministers that I know quite well and I would not object to any of them performing my service. It wouldn't bother me if David Medina, a minister and former student, who profoundly says I kicked him out of school can do my service. I'm sure people will get to the church on time since most families only print a certain number of programs with colored pictures, and I expect mine to be a keepsake. My instruction to my family is to put together a program of pictures depicting my entire adult life, not just those with all the gray hair and little or no hair. This is very important since I am being cremated and there will not be a viewing. I'm not being selfish; however, I do not want people saying, "She doesn't look like herself", "The funeral home did not do a good job", "She looks like she is just sleeping", "Didn't her body look swollen to you?", "She looks so peaceful", or "She should have been cremated."

You should get to the funeral early so that people won't have to move over so that you can squeeze in that half seat space, causing them to lose the elbow room that's so desired. You don't want to crawl over the person who came early to reserve the end seat either.

"Hello, friends, and acquaintances," I'll say. "This is my order of service. My spirit is in this room so please don't revise what I have written. This service was written with you in mind because I don't want anyone leaving, saying, 'Gosh, that sure was a long funeral.'"

Note: I'm sure there will be changes as I plan to live many years after this book is published. This is primarily for those who would like to attend my homegoing but will not be able to since they live so far away, or for those who may have to work the day my services will be held.

MARGARET B. HILL

Homegoing Services

Prelude
Processional
Song: Precious Lord
Scriptures
Acknowledgements
Resolutions (a family member will collect and read who they are from only). However, my preference, in lieu of resolutions, flowers and cards, please make a donation to Maggie's Kids Foundation, Margaret Hill Scholarship Fund at San Andreas High School, or a scholarship in my honor to any organization or university.

Obituary
Song: His Eye is on the Sparrow
Remarks: None. I don't want anything said about me that I cannot hear
Eulogy: Optional
Song: Save a Seat for Me by Otis Clay/When the Gate Swings Open by Sam Cook and the Soul Stirrers (this is the same song)
Thanks: Husband, Close family member or close friend can provide these last words
Recessional

ACKNOWLEDGEMENTS

Words cannot express the gratitude we feel toward all of our friends who have consoled us during our bereavement.

Your prayers, love, presence and your kind thoughts have sustained us. Your cards, e-mails, flowers, and gifts of food were warmly appreciated. We viewed all of the things that you have done for Margaret's family as a demonstration of God's love.

Whatever you did to console our hearts, we will always be grateful.

REMARKS

Goodbye my family and friends. I will see you on the other side. I appreciate you as much in death as I did in life and for that reason, I will say the things you probably would have said during remarks (two minutes, please).

First of all, thanks for coming out today and giving up your precious time to say farewell to me. I am so glad you found the time to give me accolades while I was alive. I appreciate all the resolutions, honors, and special recognition you gave me. Let me first give honor to God for blessing me all these years with wonderful family members and friends.

When I was young, I attended church every Sunday. Our church only met once a month so, as a family, we attended other churches as they held their once a month services. That concept has continued with me as I find myself, not becoming a member of one church, but, appreciating the Word and the good gospel music that I hear in all of them. Some might think this is a good way not to give tithes but I see it as an opportunity to give to all of God's children in many different houses. I have gone home where God has prepared a place for me and I hope that any influence that I had on your life will not be in vain. I appreciate all that you have done for me and hope I took the time to thank you when I was alive but I'm glad to have another opportunity to do so. We often say, "I feel bad because I never took the opportunity to express my appreciation to the deceased." You do not have to feel bad about that because your presence today means a lot to my family and me. It shows that you cared for me, so you are forgiven.

Remembering the words of the late Dr. Martin Luther King, Jr., should anyone ask about me and my deeds please tell them the following:

- I'm thankful to my parents who raised me on the farm and taught me to never make excuses and blame others for how I had to live.

- I'm thankful to my siblings for "having my back" whether they were sending me money while in college or encouraging me to always do my best.

- I'm thankful to my husband for his support of me and being a good cook so I didn't have to.

- I'm thankful to my cousins, nieces and nephews who looked up to me as a role model (I must have done an okay job).

- I'm thankful to my friends for accepting me as I am.

- I'm thankful to my stepchildren, step-grandchildren and step-great grandchildren who reminded me, more often than not, that patience is golden.

- I'm thankful for all the jobs I had in private industry and civil service where I was recommended for promotions and were never threatened with termination.

- I'm thankful to my neighbors who were always willing to assist in any endeavors such as putting out my garbage cans, fixing my hot water heater, and keeping an eye out when my husband sat/slept in the car in the driveway after receiving dialysis.

- I'm thankful to all my elected political friends who made it possible for me to share my vision locally, at the State level and also in Washington, DC.

- I'm thankful for the many opportunities the school district gave me to work with our young.

- I'm thankful for the many organizations of wonderful people and especially those who gave me leadership roles.

- I'm thankful to the members of my two sororities who assisted me in leadership and supported my desire to hold national offices.

- I'm thankful to my bowling buddies for all the good times at local, state and national competition.

- I'm thankful to my pinochle friends who opened their homes for the great fellowship and food as we met once a month and other times when convenient.

- I'm thankful to the writing group family who listened to me and made suggestions so that I could perfect these remarks.

- I'm very thankful to the students whose lives were touched by my involvement in their lives and theirs in mine.

- I'm thankful to all of you for understanding how much I would have appreciated the two-minute remarks that you are not making today.

- I'm thankful for the University of Redlands for giving me an honorary Doctor in the field of social justice.

- I'm thankful for having the opportunity to do an hour long interview with James Meredith, the first Black to attend an al-white college in Mississippi.

- I'm thankful for all of my federal, state, regional, county, and local awards.

- I'm thankful to all of my doctors who have treated me for everything from an ear infection to cancer.

- I'm thankful for all the students who believed me when I said you can do it and are now doing it.

- I'm thankful for the individual who is reading this because I know it is too much to put in a program.

Time is of the essence so as I say goodbye to my family and friends, I leave you with this:

I'M FREE

Don't grieve for me, for now I'm free,
I'm following the path God laid for me.

I took his hand when I heard him call,
I turned my back and left it all.

I could not stay another day,
to laugh, to love, to work or play.

Tasks left undone must stay that way,
I found that peace at the close of the day.

If my parting has left a void,
then fill it with remembered joy.

A friendship shared, a laugh, a kiss,
oh, yes these things I too, will miss.

But not burdened with times of sorrow,
I wish you the sunshine of tomorrow.

My life's been full, I've savored much,
good friends, good time, a loved one's touch.

Perhaps my time seemed all too brief,
don't lengthen it now with undue grief.

Life up your heart and share with me,
God wanted me now; He set me free.

Linda Jo Jackson

CPSIA information can be obtained
at www.ICGtesting.com
Printed in the USA
FSOW02n0402021015
11759FS